Everybody Tells Me to Be Myself but I Don't Know Who I Am

Building Your Self-Esteem

REVISED EDITION

Also by Nancy Rue

You! A Christian Girl's Guide to Growing Up
Girl Politics

Sophie's World Series

Meet Sophie (Book One)
Sophie Steps Up (Book Two)
Sophie and Friends (Book Three)
Sophie's Friendship Fiasco (Book Four)
Sophie Flakes Out (Book Five)
Sophie's Drama (Book Six)

The Lucy Series

Lucy Doesn't Wear Pink (Book One)
Lucy Out of Bounds (Book Two)
Lucy's Perfect Summer (Book Three)
Lucy Finds Her Way (Book Four)

Other books in the growing Faithgirlz!™ library

Bibles

The Faithgirlz! Bible
NIV Faithgirlz! Backpack Bible

Faithgirlz! Bible Studies

Secret Power of Love
Secret Power of Joy
Secret Power of Goodness
Secret Power of Grace

Fiction

From Sadie's Sketchbook

Shades of Truth (Book One)
Flickering Hope (Book Two)
Waves of Light (Book Three)
Brilliant Hues (Book Four)

The Girls of Harbor View

Girl Power (Book One)
Take Charge (Book Two)
Raising Faith (Book Three)
Secret Admirer (Book Four)

Boarding School Mysteries

Vanished (Book One)
Betrayed (Book Two)
Burned (Book Three)
Poisoned (Book Four)

Nonfiction

Faithgirlz Handbook
Faithgirlz Journal
Food, Faith, and Fun! Faithgirlz Cookbook
No Boys Allowed
What's a Girl to Do?
Girlz Rock
Chick Chat
Real Girls of the Bible
My Beautiful Daughter

Check out www.faithgirlz.com

faithGirlz!
the beauty of believing

Everybody Tells Me to
Be Myself
but I Don't Know Who I Am

Building Your Self-Esteem

REVISED EDITION

Nancy Rue

ZONDERVAN®

ZONDERVAN.com/
AUTHORTRACKER
follow your favorite authors

This journey is dedicated to the thirty-four mini-women on the *Tween You and Me* blog who shared their stories and questions and hopes so that your own journey can be real.

ZONDERKIDZ

Everybody Tells Me to Be Myself ... but I Don't Know Who I Am!

Copyright © 2007, 2013 by Nancy Rue

This title is also available as a Zondervan ebook.
Visit www.zondervan.com/ebooks

Illustrations copyright © 2007, 2013 by Sarah Molegraaf

Requests for information should be addressed to:
Zonderkidz, 5300 Patterson Ave. SE, Grand Rapids, Michigan 49530

Library of Congress Cataloging-in-Publication Data

Rue, Nancy N.
    Everybody tells me to be myself but I don't know who I am! / by Nancy Rue.
        p. cm.
    ISBN 978-0-310-73323-2
    1. Girls—Religious life—Juvenile literature. 2. Self-esteem in children—Religious aspects—
Christianity—Juvenile literature. I. Title.
BV4551.3.R836 2013
248.8'33—dc23   2012029589

Published in association with the literary agency of Alive Communications, Inc., 7680 Goddard Street, Suite 200, Colorado Springs, CO 80920. www.alivecommunications.com

Zonderkidz is a trademark of Zondervan.

Editor: Kim Childress
Art direction and cover design: Kris Nelson and Jody Langley
Interior Design: Sarah Molegraaf

Printed in the United States of America

13 14 15 16 17 18 19 20 21 22 /QVS/ 20 19 18 17 16 15 14 13 12 11 10 9 8 7 6 5 4 3 2

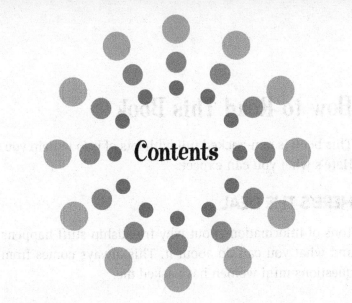

Contents

How to Read This Book. 8

1 You Want to Come Along?. 11

2 Mirror, Mirror. 35

3 Big Old Hairy Obstacles. 57

4 Talkin' Trash—Talkin' Truth 81

5 Being You—Being Her. 99

6 The Fun Part!. 123

7 Mileage Check 137

How to Read This Book

This book is jam-packed full with lots of info to help you. Here's what you can expect:

HERE'S THE DEAL

Tons of information about why friendship stuff happens and what you can do about it. This always comes from questions mini-women have asked me.

That Is SO Me

Quizzes to help you figure out where you are on things like BFFs and bullying and cliques. These are the kind of tests you don't have to study for! And no grades!

● ●

GOT GOD?

What God says about friendships and the way we need to treat other people. You'll be surprised what the Bible says about YOUR life.

● ●

YOU CAN DO IT

An artsy-craftsy way for you to try out what you've read about. And not just you, but you AND your friends. (That only makes sense, right?)

That's What I'm Talkin' About

A place for you to fill in some blanks about your own friend-ship stuff—or draw or doodle—or even journal if you really like to write and write and ... write

Mini-Women Say

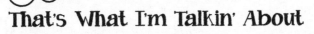Quotes from tween girls like you who say some things so much better than I can.

Just So You Know

Fun facts to make you feel smarter. (They're good things to talk about when you want to steer the conversation away from gossip!)

Who, ME?

Things you can do super fast to help you see how all this friend-information fits YOU.

Let's get started!

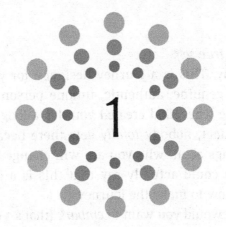

You Want to Come Along?

I have an invitation for you.

If you are a mini-woman—that is, you're a girl between the ages of eight and twelve—you're invited on a journey. It's not a *trip*, because once you set out you won't be coming back. It isn't a *vacation* either. Even though parts of it are going to be a blast for you, some of it will demand hard work. And it definitely isn't a *tour*. You'll have guides on this journey, but you'll do more than see the sights and go, "How cool is that? Now when do we eat?"

I promise you, though, that this journey will be worth your while, because where we're going is a place you really can't afford to miss out on. We're going ...

To your true self.

Seriously. This is a journey designed for you to discover the genuine, authentic, unique person you were made to be when God created you. It's a long one. As a matter of fact, nobody *totally* gets there because some of the things about who you are will change as you get older. You could actually say that this is a journey of learning how to make the journey.

So, why would you want to *embark* (that's a cool travel word for "start out") on such a tough, never-ending road? I'll let your fellow mini-women answer that for you:

> Some people at school and church think you have to act like a twenty-year-old to be cool. And sometimes I do because some of my friends are intimidating.

> Something that stops me from being me is the thought of someone not liking me or thinking I'm a freak or something.

> It's hard for me to be myself when someone is doing something better than I am.

> I don't like who I am!

> I think what keeps me from being me is that I don't know who I am in the first place.

Who, Me?

Draw a tiny frowny face next to any of those statements (or something close to them) that YOU've thought yourself.

If you've had those thoughts or others like them, that doesn't mean you're a loser. It means you're breathing. You're a tween girl, and this is the time in your life when you're finding out that ...

- You really aren't the same as everyone else.

- Not everyone automatically likes who you are.

It can be a bummer because it's happening at exactly the same time that you're discovering how much you *want* people to like who you are, especially BFFs (Best Friends Forever), CFFs (Close Friends Forever), and maybe even, uh, boys. The problem is, they're trying to figure out the same things you are. It's a wonder anybody ever gets there!

But you can. This book is like a travel guide to get you started on the journey toward your true God-made self. It's set up to help you ...

- figure out who you really-deep-down-inside are

- be that person no matter who you're with.

You may be thinking, it's easy for *me* to say you can do those two things. I'm a grown-up, after all. But I'm still on that journey, and although it's a lot easier than it used to be, there are still some bumpy roads and switchbacks along the way. And besides, I've had a lot of help with this book from mini-women who, like you, are starting out right now and are making progress. You'll see their absolutely true stories here, and you'll know you are SO not alone.

If you think you'd like to come along, let's do a little pre-journey preparation.

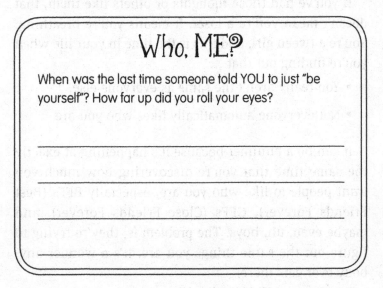

Who, ME?

When was the last time someone told YOU to just "be yourself"? How far up did you roll your eyes?

_____

_____

_____

Who, ME?

Look at the list on the next page. Draw a tiny smiley face next to each of those things YOU always, always do.

Circle the thing on that list that YOU most want to be able to do.

> **❝** I have a problem when my friends think I'm crazy and I'm just being myself. They think it's not ladylike to eat a cupcake so half of it ends up on your face. Who said I was trying to be ladylike? I'm just trying to have fun. **❞**

HERE'S THE DEAL ABOUT BEING YOURSELF

How many times have you heard grown-ups say, "Just be yourself"? Like that's supposed to prepare you for a situation where you don't know anybody, or you don't know what you're supposed to do, or you have that feeling that you are *not* going to fit in at *all*.

In the first place, what do they mean by "be yourself"? They're probably talking about a thing called *authenticity*. When you're *authentic* ...

- You're always honest.

- You don't pretend to be rich, or way smart about something, or totally into horses (or whatever everybody else is into) when you're not.

- You don't copy the way other kids dress or talk or laugh if it doesn't feel natural to you.

- You go after the things you're interested in even if nobody else does.

- You make up your own mind by what you know is good and true.

Easy, right? You just do all that stuff and you're authentic.

Uh-huh, except for these questions your fellow mini-women ask:

❝ What if I'm so honest I hurt people's feelings? **❞**

❝ What if I just do my thing and everybody thinks I'm weird? **❞**

❝ What if I always do what's right and nobody wants to be with me because I'm too 'good'? **❞**

❝ What if I don't even know what I like and what I'm interested in and how I want to dress? What about that? **❞**

❝ Certain people keep me from feeling like I can be myself. Mean people. My family sometimes. That so-cute boy I have a crush on. **❞**

Take a big ol' sigh of relief. The whole point of this journey is to turn every one of those "what ifs" into a "what is." It *is* possible to ...

- Be honest and encouraging at the same time.
- Know what your own "unique thing" is and go for it without worrying about other kids thinking you're weird.
- Show people that *good* is cool.

16

- Discover more and more the special, one-of-a-kind person you are ... and love yourself.

Wait ... did I just say you're going to love yourself? Isn't that conceited? Selfish? Stuck up?

Let's see what God has to say about that. Read this next part very carefully, because without it, the journey can't even begin.

● ●

GOT GOD?

Even if you've only just started thinking about God on your own (as in, outside of Sunday school class), you probably know that God-loving people believe God thought each one of us up, made us, and put us here for a reason. The Bible (which is where God mostly talks to us) says that over and over. Here's just one example:

> [God] has shaped each person in turn; now he watches everything we do.
>
> Psalm 33:15 THE MESSAGE

It's kind of cool to imagine God's magnificent hands making an individual person who is totally different from every other baby girl or boy ever created before. It's like God is a potter, shaping people out of clay. God makes a perfect work of art, breathes life into it, and loves it.

> "Woe to those who quarrel with their Maker ... Does the clay say to the potter, 'What are you making?'"
>
> Isaiah 45:9

So if God loves what God has made, including you, how can you do any less than love yourself too?

It's hard, though, with the world telling you to pick yourself apart all the time:

○ Are your clothes hip?

○ Is your slang up to date?

○ Are you cool enough?

○ Funny enough?

○ Blond enough?

We'll talk more about that later. For now, just remember that God knows how hard it is, which is why God sent Jesus to make everything way, way clear. From all the commandments the people had to remember and follow, Jesus got it down to the two most important ones:

> "'Love the Lord your God with all your heart and with all your soul and with all your mind.' This is the first and greatest commandment. And the second is like it: 'Love your neighbor as yourself.'"
>
> Matthew 22:37–39

Basically, if you don't love yourself, you're not going to be very good at loving other people. Loving yourself does NOT mean you're conceited. In fact, loving your true self is actually a requirement. Jesus goes on to say that all the other commandments are based on these two. If you can't love God with everything you have—and love yourself and other people the same way—you don't have a chance of obeying "Honor your father and your mother" (Exodus

20:12) or "Do not envy" or any of the rest of them. That could get to be a mess.

Here's the way it works in *God's* world:

- God made you beautifully unique, right down to your fingerprints, your one-of-a-kind voice, and your designer ears.

- God gave you made-for-you talents and interests (and not just the kind that show up on *American Idol*).

- God shows you who you are as you get to know him better and better. That is, in fact, the only way to know the Unique You.

It only makes sense, then, that if you hate who you are and try to be something or someone else, you grow more false. You move further *away* from your true, beautiful self.

Not only that, but anytime you reject any part of your real self—maybe the fact that you're naturally quiet or you have a crazy sense of humor—you're also telling God he didn't know what he was doing when he created you.

I mean, really?

● ●

That Is So Me!

So what do you say we start down the path to the Unique You right now.

Since one of the most important signs of an authentic person is honesty, here's a chance to practice that. Be totally truthful with yourself as you take this quiz. There are no right or wrong answers, no passing or failing. Your score just tells you where you're starting from—sort of like the You Are Here star on the directory at the mall.

After reading each situation listed, circle the letter of the choice that sounds the most like you.

- If I got to decorate my room any way I wanted, I would ...

  A. immediately know exactly how I'd have it.

  B. look at pictures and at my friends' rooms and come up with my own combination.

  C. find a picture in a magazine and have mine just like that.

- If my mom packed raw veggies in my school lunch, I would ...

  A. not eat them because I've tried them and I can't stand them (or I'd gobble them down because I love them).

  B. eat them only if someone else at my table would eat some.

  C. throw them away because it isn't cool to eat veggies when everybody else has pizza and French fries.

- If I could give myself a different name, I would ...

  A. choose a nickname that fits my personality. How cool would that be?

  B. try on some different names to see how other people liked them before I decided; I think it would be kinda fun.

C. name myself after somebody famous; I might still be a little nervous that somebody would laugh at it, though.

- If I had to design a logo (trademark) for myself as a class assignment, I would ...

A. love that assignment!

B. be kind of stressed about it until I saw what other people were doing.

C. ask the teacher if I could just answer the questions at the end of the chapter.

- If I were asked what color I would use to describe myself, I would say ...

A. "Hel-lo-o. My favorite, of course!"

B. " ... Um, give me a minute to think ..."

C. "What? How am I supposed to know that? I am so over this quiz."

Remember that your score just tells you where you are as you start the Unique You journey, and that makes it so much easier to figure out which way you have to go to get where you want to be.

Count up your A's, B's, and C's.

On the map below, put a star (*) on whichever point fits you: mostly A's, mostly B's, or mostly C's.

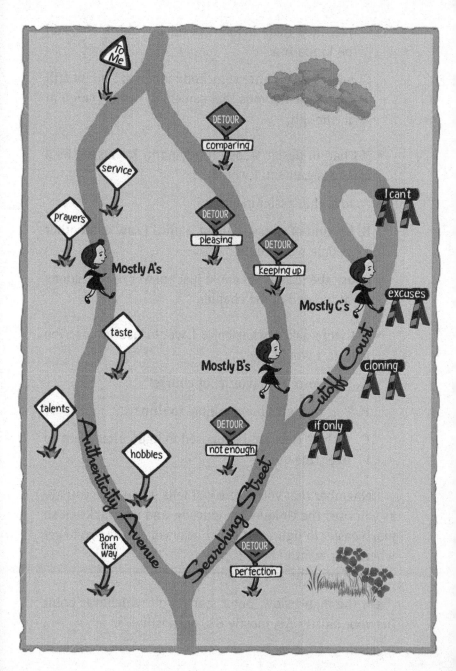

If you have more A's than other letters, you're already on the road to becoming your authentic self. You know a lot about yourself, and what you don't know you're finding out. You're about to discover fun ways to learn more and get help in avoiding wrong turns and dead ends.

If you have more B's than other letters, you're searching for a way to be yourself. Right now you may be looking to other people to find out what's cool, what helps you fit in. Even though you may gather information and then make your own decisions, you're about to learn how to depend less and less on what other people think and more on what *you* know is true about yourself. You're off to a good start.

If you have more C's than other letters, just being yourself might be a little scary for you right now. Don't give up and say you're a born wimp. Take a breath, say a prayer, and keep reading. You'll find out how to shake off the "Who Am I's?" and get right to Authenticity Avenue. It's actually a fun journey, and once you're on it, you'll wonder why you were ever afraid.

No matter where you are as you start on this adventure, you can still get to yourself—your true God-made self. Even if you're on your way to a dead end on Cutoff Court right now, you can make a U-turn this very minute. All you have to do is keep reading and following the path.

> 66 The world makes it hard to be who I am, you know what I mean? It's like everyone expects you to have a boyfriend at twelve and wear makeup and stuff. And I don't. 99

Who, ME?

What was the last thing YOU did that you didn't want to do but you did it because everybody else did?

_____

_____

_____

Who, ME?

Name one thing YOU would do if you didn't think people would laugh at you.

_____

_____

_____

" Sometimes I feel like I have to do what some of my friends do, especially some new friends I don't know too well. It's sometimes like I have to do what they do to be friends with them, even if they SAY they want me to be myself. **"**

Who, ME?

What is one "requirement" someone has for YOU that just doesn't fit you?

_____

_____

_____

❝ I sometimes hate myself so much that it flows out to other people, and I end up hurting them. **❞**

❝ Most of the time I am myself, but I don't always feel at ease doing it. **❞**

Who, ME?

When do YOU feel the most uncomfortable around people?

_____

_____

_____

HERE'S THE DEAL ABOUT NOT MAKING THE JOURNEY

What if you don't make the journey? What if it's easier to be who other people tell you to be?

There are several answers to that question. Before we start out for real, let's find out why it's dangerous to not make the journey at all. Below are just a few of the things that can happen if you're not being your authentic self.

- **You do things you really don't want to do.** Most teasing, lying, and gossiping doesn't happen because people want to be mean. It starts because somebody's unhappy with herself or she needs attention or she wants to feel important. If you're just being you, you're usually happy, you get the right kind of attention, and you know you're valuable.

- **You don't do things you really want to do.** For instance, you might miss out on some really cool art classes if it's more important to you that *other* people won't think they're cool. And that's not all. You might fail to stand up for somebody who's being teased or fail to stand up *to* someone who's bullying you because you're not sure if your group will approve. Always checking to see if you still fit can really cheat you out of the places and things and people who are perfect for you.

- **You get resentful about always having to "measure up."** Doing your best in school and at home and following the right rules—all that helps build your confidence. But if your friends (or the people you want to be friends with) also have "requirements" for belonging to the group—beyond being yourself—you're bound to start thinking little mean thoughts and snapping at people and generally feeling like you want to smack somebody. And for some reason, the person you say something evil to is seldom the person you're really annoyed with. Yeah, it's a problem.

- **You never feel totally comfortable.** When it's not easy to just be you, nervous questions wave their sweaty hands in your head. "Do I look okay?" "Did I just laugh too loud?" "Do I sound like a geek when I say that?" "If I do this, will they still be my friends?" "I don't know how to act right now!" Pretty soon you're chewing on your fingernails or your hair or your pencils while the questions keep chewing on *you* from the inside.

- **As you get older, that anxiety can get more serious.** Some girls develop eating disorders like anorexia or bulimia. Some injure themselves on purpose. Some get depressed. Others always seem to be angry. Still others just load themselves up with activities so they won't have to think about it. None of that makes growing up fun, and a lot of it is downright dangerous.

- **If you lose the Unique You that God made you to be, you won't discover what God has planned for you to do with your life.** No one who is being her honest, genuine self ever has to worry that she won't figure out what God wants her to do. She'll just naturally do it. But a girl who tries to be somebody else or a different somebody for every group she's with may never find her purpose. That's where the real happiness is, in living out exactly what you were put here for. It would be such a bummer to miss that.

Who, ME?

What's one dream YOU have for your life that feels pretty real to you?

_____

_____

_____

GOT GOD? (AGAIN)

As you go forward on the path to your God-made self, remember this passage, written by John about Christ:

> Whoever did want him,
> who believed he was who he claimed
> and would do what he said,
> He made to be their true selves,
> their child-of-God selves.

> John 1:12 THE MESSAGE

Let's make that our journey verse. Keep it in your mind that God made you to be his child. Jesus was—and still is—the *perfect* child of God, and he's the only one we should imitate, just by following his lead.

If you've got that, then let's go for it!

> **❝**You have to find you buried underneath everything people tell you about yourself.**❞**

> **❝**Other people have this image of me. I'm shy around people I don't know, so they think I'm always quiet. They imagine things about me from the outside, but most of the time they aren't true. It's just that I have two sides of me. One side likes to study, get good grades, and read books. But the other side likes to have fun, sing, listen to music, dance, and spend time with friends. I have to work on not getting trapped in the image that other people have of me.**❞**

YOU CAN DO IT

At the end of each *leg* of your journey (*leg* is another cool travel word for "part") in this book, you'll have a chance to do an activity that will help you get to know and be yourself even more. On this leg, discover what you *already* know about yourself deep inside by making a *collage*. That's a collection of magazine images (or photographs, if that's okay with your mom) that you paste together on poster board or paper to create one big picture. We'll take it step by step.

What you'll need:

○ a pile of magazines you're allowed to cut pictures from (Be SURE to ask permission before you start.)

29

○ scissors (or you can tear pictures out.)

○ paste or glue (Tape doesn't work so well.)

○ a piece of cardboard, poster board, or paper at least 11 inches by 14 inches

○ a timer (or just a clock or watch you can see easily)

○ a quiet place where you can think and spread things out and not be interrupted (by pesky brothers, nosy sisters, mischievous pets ...)

How to make it happen:

○ Set your timer for twenty minutes (or look at the clock or watch and jot down what time you start).

○ During that twenty minutes, go through the magazines. Each time you come to a picture or some words you really like, cut or tear them out. You don't have to have a reason to choose a picture or words other than "I just like it!"

○ When twenty minutes have passed, put the magazines aside and spread all the cut-out pictures and words on your paper. Rearrange them, sides touching, until they create a picture that makes you go, "That's me!" You don't have to be able to explain why you placed the images that way—it just has to make you happy.

○ Glue or paste the images to the paper the way you've arranged them.

○ Sit back from your completed collage and gaze at it.

○ Rather than looking at each picture and word individually, look at the whole collage as if it were one big picture.

○ Try to come up with one sentence that describes the picture. *This is a picture of a person who* _____. For example:

› This is a picture of a person who is upbeat and cheerful and loves life.

› This is a picture of a person who likes to be quiet and peaceful.

› This is a picture of a person who has a lot of different sides to her personality, from totally wacky to way smart.

○ If you need help discovering your sentence, think about ...

› *The colors.* Are they bright and wild? Soft and pastel? Black and white? What do the colors tell you about your personality that you know is totally the truth?

› *The way you've placed things on the page.* Is it neat and orderly? Scattered and happily confused? Does it make a design? What does your placement tell you about the way you do things that is absolutely right on?

› *The kinds of pictures you chose.* Are they all of one kind of thing? Is there a huge variety? Are they in categories? What does that tell you about your talents and interests and tastes—the ones you may even keep secret from other people?

○ Put your collage up in a place where you can see it as you continue your journey.

○ Look at it often. See what more it might tell you. (I know it's weird, but it does kind of "speak" to you.)

○ If there is someone in your life who always accepts you for who you are, ask him or her to look at your collage and tell you what they see. You still get to decide if that helps you know yourself even better.

○ Let your collage help you *like* the real you more and more.

That's What I'm Talkin' About!

Here are some things you can write down or draw as you consider that collage of yours.

One thing I see that I didn't know before about myself: __

_____

_____

_____

_____.

One thing I see that is exactly who I thought I was: _____

_____

_____

_____

_____.

One thing I can't figure out about myself is: _____

_____

_____

_____

_____.

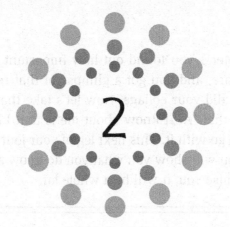

Mirror, Mirror

When I posted on the *Tween You and Me* blog that I was going to write a new book about being who you really are, comments like this one filled my inbox:

"Lately I don't know who I am. Yeah, it's sad. I have been such a jerk. I've been acting like one of those girls who is so spoiled and bratty. I've been mean to my little brother and said stuff I'm sorry about, and I know it's because I feel like a stranger to myself. I need help finding me."

Several mini-women echoed that, and one girl posted:

"All I know about me is that I like polka dots."

Well, that's a start.

Seriously, it is.

In chapter 1 you found out how important it is to be who you are, and you got a glimpse of that real person when you did your collage. Now let's take that glimpse, that hint, that "All I know about me is that I like polka dots," and go with it. This next leg of your journey to the Unique You will show you what you do know about you, and I promise you, it will be a whole lot.

Who, ME?

Name the first thing that pops into your head that you absolutely know about yourself.

_____

_____

That Is SO Me!

We'll start with some basic details. As always, be completely honest. Don't worry about sounding conceited—we already went there, remember? Simply fill in the blanks with the truth.

1. Sit or stand in front of a mirror and take a good, long look at the girl staring back at you. Make some faces at her if you want to. Put on your sad expression. Your jazzed one. Your terrified one. Your silliest ones. Show every side of yourself.

2. Write down five words that describe the personality

of the girl YOU see in the mirror, not the one some-one else tells you that you are or should be (examples: friendly, quiet, eager, timid, creative, sassy).

3. Think of one thing you like *least* about your personality and write it down (even if you've included it on the list above).

4. **Think of one thing you like *most* about your personality and write it down (even if you've already included it above).**

5. Write down three things you often hear people say about you (whether they're negative or positive, and whether you think they're true or not).

6. Ask your mom (or someone else who always accepts you for who you are) to tell you ...

  ‣ two words to describe your personality.

  ‣ the thing she likes most about you.

  ‣ one thing about you she thinks you should work on.

Look over the descriptions you've just written. Think about the following questions. You can write your answers or just chat with yourself about them in your head.

1. What things on your list make you unique? (Even if you think that's the same as strange or weird!) Put a star next to each of those.

2. Does your list sound like the you that you know?

———

3. Were there any surprises, things you hadn't thought of before? _____

4. Do other people appear to know the real you? _____

5. Are you different from other people in your family? _____

6. Are you way different from your friends or the people you want to be friends with? _____

Who, ME?

Name one thing YOU want to turn UP about yourself.

_____

Name one thing you want to turn DOWN.

_____

Who, ME?

What's YOUR most frequent put-down of yourself?

_____

_____

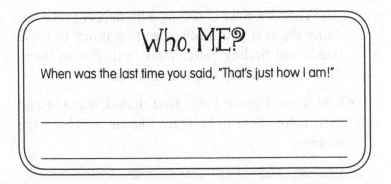

Who, ME?

When was the last time you said, "That's just how I am!"

_____

_____

HERE'S THE DEAL ABOUT THE "NEGATIVES"

> **"**What if there's stuff on that list that I really can't stand about myself? Do I have to just say, 'Oh, well, that's me'?**"**

Along the way you're in for some fun surprises, but you may also discover a few things about yourself that maybe you aren't so crazy about. That, of course, is because nobody's perfect and all our lives we have things to work on. Here are a few things to "pack" in your mind for the journey:

- Life is one long process of turning *up* the volume of our best qualities and turning it *down* on our weak places. Eventually your strengths will drown out those funky places most of the time.

- DO NOT PUT YOURSELF DOWN for having faults. Just work on them.

- This book will help you.

- Being bratty, bossy, or mean isn't how anybody just

"is." They are ways of coping with deeper problems. Being the real you involves getting down to those issues and finding better ways to deal with them. This book will help you with that too.

• God doesn't make junk. God makes humans and then helps them to be more like he is. That's the journey.

Who, ME?

Does race or culture play a part in who YOU are?

_____

_____

_____

Who, ME?

Name one way YOU are different from the girls you know.

_____

_____

_____

Who, ME?

Name one way YOU are different from this time last year.

_____

_____

Who, ME?

Does anyone say to YOU, "You're just like so-and-so?"

_____

_____

Who, ME?

What's YOUR strongest talent? (Yes, you have at least one!)

_____

_____

HERE'S THE DEAL ABOUT WHAT YOU START WITH

66 My mom is always saying, 'You're just like your father,' and I don't think she means in a good way. What am I supposed to do with that? 99

You don't get to just make yourself up as you go along. Certain basics come with the You Package.

- **Race**—If you explore the history of your race or culture, you might be amazed at how it explains pieces of yourself. You're headed for confusion if you try to deny your beginnings. Instead, be proud that you're African American or of Asian descent or have a Hispanic or Swedish or Dutch or other ethnic background.

- **Gender**—Being a girl has its own special characteristics. Studies of the brain show that women multitask (do a lot of different things at the same time) better than men, and we can go back and forth from our creative side to our logical side more easily too. You'll love this: Girls usually mature faster than boys (which is why some boys your age seem like absurd little creeps right now!).

- **Age**—If you're eight or nine or ten, you probably like facts and learning cool information about science, animals, history—stuff like that. If you're eleven or twelve, you might be thinking about things like feelings, opinions, and why people do what they do.

Some of the things you care about now will change as you get older. Your age will always be an important part of knowing yourself and how you're growing.

- **Family**—Some of our unique qualities are inherited. Does anyone ever say that you are just like your mother? Maybe you have a quick temper like your dad or the same sense of humor as a great-grandfather you never even met. That doesn't mean you can shrug and say, "I guess I'm doomed." It's just good to be aware of whether these qualities need to be turned down or cranked up. If you're adopted, you really don't know, so just claim all your characteristics as totally you and take responsibility for them.

- **Talents**—God gives every one of us a gift. It might not be a rockin' singing voice or a kick-buns pitching arm, but it's something God needs you to use to make the world better or to let people see him. Can you get people laughing without even trying? Are you amazing with little kids? Do you have more energy than any two other girls put together? Can you sense your mom's mood the minute you walk in the door? Finding your gift is the best part of self-discovery.

- **Tastes**—Why is it that some babies love their first bite of applesauce and others spit it out? Why did you have a favorite color when you were two? Why does one identical twin love rap, while the other is crazy over country music? Because we're all born with certain likes and dislikes. Yeah, some tastes are developed as you grow up (very few three-year-olds dig stuffed mushrooms or the opera). But some are just woven into that marvelous creature known as you.

Who, ME?

YOUR fave color _____

Fave pizza toppings _____

Fave kind of music _____

All-time fave book or movie or computer game

_____

Who, ME?

How would YOU be different if YOU lived someplace else?

_____

_____

_____

_____

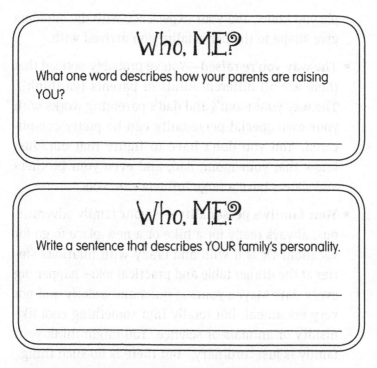

Who, ME?

What one word describes how your parents are raising YOU?

_____

Who, ME?

Write a sentence that describes YOUR family's personality.

_____

HERE'S THE DEAL ABOUT HOW YOU'RE GROWING UP

What we've been talking about is *nature*. The other basic that shapes who you are is called *nurture*. How you're growing up is part of the You Package.

• **Where you live**—Your community helps shape you from the moment you're born into it. Living in a crowded city might make you bold and unafraid or careful and suspicious. If you're growing up in a small town, you may not have much fear of other people, or you may be very private because everybody in town knows everybody else's business. The opportunities you have in your little world, the people you know, and your experience with the outdoors give shape to the personality you arrived with.

- **The way you're raised**—You've probably noticed that there are all different kinds of parents (ya think!). The way your mom's and dad's parenting works with your own special personality can be pretty complicated, and you don't have to figure that out. Just know that your mom, dad, and even your brothers and sisters have a huge influence on you.

- **Your family's personality**—Is your family adventurous, always ready for a hike or a new place to go for vacation? Or is it wild and crazy with hilarious stories at the dinner table and practical jokes happening every day? Maybe yours is quiet and orderly and not very emotional, but totally into something cool like history or animals or science. You might think your family is just "ordinary," but there is no such thing.

- **Religion**—How deep your family's faith is has TONS to do with how you use your basic qualities. A faith community full of love and acceptance that guides you instead of just giving you the rules helps you grow into a loving, confident woman of integrity. You can still become that person without the community, but it's easier when you have support. So start praying for that now. God's there for you, no matter what.

Who, ME?

How would YOU be different if YOU went to another church or didn't have a church?

_____

_____

_____

Who, ME?

What's YOUR dream hobby?

_____

_____

Who, ME?

What's one activity YOU would really enjoy (or already do)? Name one thing it says about YOU.

_____

_____

_____

> **"**All I know is the person I am does not include playing the piano, sharing a room with my sisters, or not having a cell phone.**"**

HERE'S THE DEAL ABOUT THE CHOICES YOU MAKE

> **"**Sometimes it seems like all I can do is what everybody tells me to, only they don't understand that's not ME!**"**

Don't think that all of who you are is already decided for you. Your own decisions help shape the You Package too.

- **Hobbies**—What you want to do in your free time tells you a lot about your true self. Can you spend hours at your personal activities and be surprised that so much time has gone by? That's a you thing. Your hobby (or one you'd like to have) tells you that you're sporty, artistic, musical, organized, curious, or just about anything cool you can name. Whenever you do something that gives you joy, you learn something about yourself.

- **Organized activities**—What do your after-school choices tell you about you? Sports might say you're athletic, competitive, or a team player. The arts could be telling you you're creative or emotional. Clubs may whisper that you're a leader, a joiner, or that you like to serve. Even choosing no organized activities at all could be saying you're independent, a thinker, or a free spirit. Not liking something can speak volumes about you too.

- **The people you're with**—Who you choose for friends can tell you a whole bunch about yourself. Ask yourself these questions:

  › Who are your closest friends? Or who do you want to be close friends with?

  › Why do you like being with them?

  › Do you try to be like them? Why?

  › Who do you try to impress?

  › When is it hard being with your friends?

  › Is there a teacher or a coach who seems to get who you really are?

  › Is there an adult you want to be like when you get to be one?

  › Is there someone in your class who reminds you of yourself?

  › Is there a grown-up besides your parents you feel comfortable talking to?

  › Do you know a boy who doesn't drive you nuts?

We're drawn to people because we see in them what we like about ourselves. The people you admire and feel relaxed with can show you some things about who you are. People you feel shy and awkward with can show you who you aren't! (And remember, that's okay.)

That's a lot to think about. It can even seem like hard

work. You're only going to do that hard work if you know why it's way important. Let's make a stop on our journey and check in with God.

● ●

GOT GOD?

Why does God want you to see yourself so clearly?

> [God] has saved us and called us to a holy life—not because of anything we have done but because of his own purpose and grace.
>
> 2 Timothy 1:9

The verse says God had a reason for making you, so obviously it's pretty important for you to discover what that is. Here's how Jesus said it:

> "No one lights a lamp and puts it in a place where it will be hidden, or under a bowl. Instead they put it on its stand, so that those who come in may see the light.
>
> Luke 11:33

Jesus was an amazing storyteller because he used things people were familiar with to help explain stuff that might be hard to understand. We aren't necessarily acquainted with lighting a lamp and putting it on a stand (we have light switches now!), so let's try something Jesus might use if he were trying to make his point today:

"Girl, don't become a reclining chair that burps."

Seriously. And he might go on with something like this:

"Imagine this kind of life for your future.

"The alarm clock rings in the morning. You stumble to the bathroom, you scare yourself awake with the reflection of a baggy-eyed, frown-faced woman in the mirror.

"Somehow you get yourself dressed and drag yourself out to your old beat-up car. You're going to be late for work. Again.

"You take your place and you do the same task you do every day, over and over. Your stomach growls because you didn't have time for breakfast. You look at your watch to see if it's lunchtime.

"It's 8:02.

"You must look at your watch fifteen hundred times that day, wishing it would be five o'clock. When it finally is, you drive home, drag yourself into the house, flop into your favorite reclining chair, and yell, 'Hey, babe! Order a pizza!'

"Your husband orders a pizza while you pick up the remote and flip through the channels. The pizza arrives—greasy and salty and practically cold—and you eat a couple of pieces that taste like greasy, salty cardboard.

"You lean back in your reclining chair, open your mouth, and let a big ol' belch rip through the room. Your husband says, 'Good one.'

"After that, you go to bed, get up the next morning, and do the same thing. Day after day after day ...

"Is that the kind of life you want, my Princess?" Jesus might say. "Because that's not what the Father had in mind when he created you. God gave you a unique place in this world so you can help people see him. Are you doing that living in a recliner that occasionally erupts with a burp?

"Don't live like that! Get out there and show 'em what you're workin' with: a bursting-with-life spirit with a reason for being here."

That pretty much says it all, doesn't it?

● ●

YOU CAN DO IT

Ready to find out more about your true self every day? One of the best ways to do that—and it's been used by people (especially women) since paper was invented—is through **journaling**.

Keeping a journal means writing in a special blank book every day—or at least regularly. It's a way to express your feelings, work out problems, vent about stuff that's driving you bonkers, and describe things that are happening in your life. If you would rather have a tooth pulled—without any Novocain—than write when you don't have to, maybe these will make the idea seem more acceptable to you:

- You don't have to worry about spelling, grammar, or punctuation because nobody's ever going to read your journal except you.

- You can write anything you want. Anything.

- You can also draw pictures, write poems and songs, or just plain doodle … as long as it's all about you and your life.

- You can create your own code if you want to. Use fake names for the people you write about (just in case somebody else—like a sibling who can't stay out of your stuff—does read it). Use secret words for certain feelings. It's yours, so you can do whatever you want. Really.

Recording things in your journal is like having a private room where you can say anything and nobody tells you you're a moron. If that seems weird, write to a pal of your own creation in your journal. Better yet, write to God. Even if you write only a couple of lines a day, you'll start to look forward to it.

To make your journal even more personal and fun, create your own. You can decorate a plain notebook, but if you want it to be really, really you, try this:

What you'll need:

- ○ a piece of 8½" x 11" heavy paper or poster board for the cover
- ○ at least twenty sheets of blank filler paper no bigger than the cover
- ○ 30" of ribbon, yarn, or twine
- ○ a heavy-duty hole punch
- ○ anything you want to decorate it with (glitter, stickers, beads, felt, whatever says YOU!)

How to make it happen:

1. Fold the cover as exactly in half as you can.

2. Mark three places to punch holes along the folded edge (about ½ inch from edge).

3. Punch three holes in the cover.

4. Fold all the filler paper in half together.

5. Place it inside the cover and mark with a pencil where to punch holes in the paper.

6. Punch the holes in the filler paper. (You might have to do this two or three sheets at a time if your hole punch won't go through all of them.)

7. Put the filler paper inside the cover so the holes line up.

8. Feed your ribbon, yarn, or twine through the center hole until it's halfway through.

9. Bring the end that's on the bottom of the journal up through the top hole.

10. Bring the end that's coming up from the middle hole down through the bottom hole.

11. Bring the end that's now on the bottom of the journal up through the center hole.

12. Both ends should be on the front cover side of the journal. Tie them together in a knot, and then make a pretty bow or whatever. You can trim the ends if you want.

13. Decorate the cover so that it's totally YOU.

Keep your journal in a special hidden place so no one will be tempted to read it. If you think somebody might get into it, you won't be as honest with yourself.

• Tell your mom you're keeping a journal and ask her to support you in protecting your privacy.

- If parents object to you writing things you don't want them to read, share this chapter with them. Better yet, make each of them a journal. Sometimes it takes a journaler to understand a journaler.

- Try to write in your journal at the same time every day. If you can't do that, come as close as you can.

- It's fun to have special pens to write with. Try different colors for different moods or subjects. Or use black for writing and colors for doodling and decorating. This is your special time and place. Make it as totally the Unique You as possible.

- If you just write about what you did during the day, it might get boring once in a while. Most of us don't have thrilling experiences every minute. But if you write about how you feel about something that's going on—or describe one thing that really got you angry, or sad, or overjoyed—it will always be interesting. It's a much better way to get to know yourself.

- It's also fun to write about your hopes and dreams, about how you want things to go—even just the next day. Nothing is too silly to put on paper. And even if it is "silly," what's wrong with that?

- If you hate to write, just choose one word for the day, write it really big on your page, and then decorate it. You'll still be thinking about your day and your feelings while you're doing it.

That's What I'm Talkin' About!

Here are some things you can write or draw in that new journal of yours:

The BEST thing I discovered about ME when I read this chapter was _____

_____

I've figured out that being _____

_____

isn't really who I am. It's just how I cope with _____

_____

I always thought it was lame to be _____

_____

_____,

but now I don't think so because _____

_____

_____

_____.

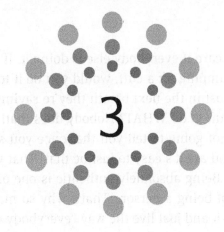

Big Old Hairy Obstacles

One of your fellow mini-women wrote this to me in an e-mail:

"It seems like every time I think of something I'm really excited about and I tell people, my mom says, 'That's nice. Do you have homework?' and my sister tells me I probably can't do it because of this, this, or this, and my friends look at me like I just grew a second nose or something. So I'm like, maybe who I am is just lame."

Yeah, figuring out who you are is one thing. *Being* that in a world where everybody has an opinion is something else entirely. One minute somebody is saying this to you:

"I don't care if everybody else is doing it. If everybody else was jumping off a cliff, would you do it too?"

But almost in the next breath they're saying:

"You want to do WHAT? Nobody does that!"

So I'm not going to tell you that once you start learning who you are it's easy to just be that. That would be a big fat lie. Being absolutely authentic is one of the hardest parts of being a person. That's why so many people give up on it and just live the way "everybody else" does. And sometimes that does mean jumping off a cliff, in a way. It's one of the reasons kids get involved in drugs and drinking and cheating and ... well, the list goes on.

This next leg of the journey will bring us to some of the roadblocks you'll come up against as you travel your path. Knowing what they look like and how to knock them down will help you stay on track with the real you.

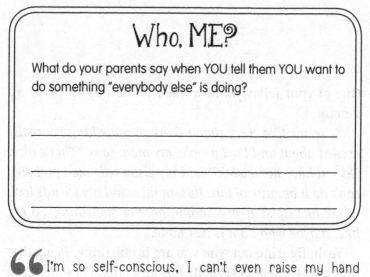

Who, ME?

What do your parents say when YOU tell them YOU want to do something "everybody else" is doing?

_____

_____

_____

❝I'm so self-conscious, I can't even raise my hand unless someone tells me to.❞

Who, ME?

Draw a frowny face next to any thing that YOU have done like these mini women.

66 When I'm feeling like I don't belong, I don't know whether to just be quiet or try to put myself out there more. Some people say, 'Do you ever talk?' Then I feel worse. 99

66 What makes it hard for me to be myself is when people insult the way my family does things. We're different, but 'different' isn't the same as 'untouchable!' 99

Who, ME?

When do YOU feel like you're supposed to be perfect?

_____

_____

66 I have Attention Deficit Hyperactivity Disorder (ADHD) so I'm almost always really hyper, but I don't tell people at school that so they don't think I'm a freak, but then

they say, 'Why can't you just act normal?' So I don't feel like I can be me except when I'm home alone. **"**

Who, ME?

When do YOU feel like you're not good enough?

_____

_____

_____

" If only I could find something I'm good at besides school. Nobody cares if I'm smart if I can't play a sport or an instrument or something. **"**

Who, ME?

What is one way YOU are different around adults and friends?

_____

_____

_____

66 My mom and dad always say I'm too girly-girl, but I don't know how to be anything else, so I always feel wrong. **99**

Who, ME?

What's one way YOU think you might be "too much"?

_____

_____

Who, ME?

Where do YOU try to "keep up"?

_____

_____

66 Everyone at school is reading all the new books and seeing the vampire movies, and when they ask me about it, I just kind of act normal and pretend I know what they're talking about. I have to do that to even feel halfway included. **99**

HERE'S THE DEAL WITH BIG OLD HAIRY OBSTACLES

The roadblocks we're talking about aren't flimsy barricades you can just crash through. They seem more like gigantic hairy monsters that make you think it's pointless to even try. These fanged creatures can actually make you ...

- wear a style you feel ridiculous in because all the other girls are wearing it.

- practically change your whole personality to fit in.

- snub somebody you actually like because the other girls you're with don't like her.

- not raise your hand in class even though you know the answer because the other kids might think you're a show-off or a brainiac.

- Hide your feelings so nobody will know what's really going on inside you.

Those Big Old Hairy Obstacles—or BOHOs—become even more powerful when you are ...

- trying to impress somebody.

- longing to be part of a certain group, no matter what it takes.

- dying for attention.

- trying to be invisible.

The BOHOs can actually make you think you have to do things like ...

- Tell a lie so you won't feel like a weirdo.

- Pretend you know what everybody's discussing even though you're totally clueless.

- Blurt out something totally bizarre when one of the "in" girls suddenly starts talking to you.

- Completely clam up until somebody asks you if you even *know* how to talk.

When we first start realizing that BOHOs are getting in our way, we tend to think they're other people. You know, like …

- **The "popular" girls,** who seem to have the power to say what's cool to wear and say and do and think.

- **The boys,** who can be so obnoxious in pointing out everybody's "differences" (while at the same time making that disgusting noise with their armpits and burping the alphabet).

- **The bullies,** who make it unsafe to attract any attention at all.

- **Your siblings,** who just can't let anything go.

- **Your parents,** who sometimes just want you to follow the rules and not make waves.

- **The whole world,** which is always using its ads and TV shows and movies to tell you who you're supposed to be.

Yeah, those things can seem pretty big and hairy, especially because there are always going to be "popular people" and guys and the world with its messed-up messages. But they aren't the real obstacles. The things that actually block the road for each of us are *inside* us. And that's good news because those things you *can* get rid of.

First, let's expose them for the frauds they are.

BOHO #1. Thinking you have to be perfect. Even when you're just being yourself, you're bound to make mistakes. But here's a news flash: You're going to make even *more* mistakes if you're always asking...

- **What if** I make some weird noise when I'm laughing?

- **What if** I spill something on my outfit? Or get lettuce stuck in my teeth and nobody tells me?

- **What if** I say something lame? What if I can't think of anything to say at all?

- **What if** I ask too many questions? What if I don't ask enough? What if I ask the wrong ones?

Those are the "What Ifs." Here's "What IS":

- **You're not perfect, and you never will be.** Thinking you have to be perfect either (a) makes you always feel like you're not good enough or (b) makes you want to give up before you try. Neither of those gets you anywhere.

- **Nobody else is perfect either.** Not the girls in the "in-crowd." Not the cute boy. Not your big sister everybody says you should be like. Nobody.

- **You can only grow to be "perfectly yourself,"** and even then you're still going to make mistakes.

- **The closest you can get to perfect is to pour out love** ... on God, on other people, and on yourself.

BOHO #2—Thinking that your true self isn't good enough. You can go nuts with the questions, right?

- **What if** I do my best, but I still only get B's and my parents want me to make A's?

- **What if** the group of girls I want to belong to doesn't like who I am when I'm not being like them?

- **What if** I'm totally myself in school, and my teachers think I'm strange or a troublemaker?

- **What if** I try out for a sport or a play or something and I don't make it?

You can probably add a few of your own "What Ifs." But here's "What IS":

- Everyone is good at something, but nobody is good at everything.

- There is at least one good friend—and probably tons of them—for a truly authentic person. Your friends **are** the cool kids because they're your friends, not because they get voted "Most Popular."

- Most people love to be around somebody who's totally real—someone they can trust.

- Anybody who rejects you for not being her clone wasn't meant to be your friend. At least not until she discovers **her** real self.

Now, yes, there are certain people who have some control in your life these days. Parents. Teachers. Coaches. They have a lot to say about what you can and can't *do*, but even they can't determine who you *are*. That doesn't have to be an issue if you follow two "Rules of the Road":

- **Rule 1. It may be that you'll have to turn down the volume on your "realness" when you're around them**. Maybe tone down your big laugh or save your mischievous sense of humor for later when you're just with your friends.

- **Rule 2.** Remember that **no adult should ever force you to do something you aren't able to do or don't believe in.** If you're in that situation, ask your parents or another grown-up you trust to help you.

BOHO #3: Thinking that your true self is way too much. The questions can bug you like a mosquito in the dark ...

- **What if** I give the right answers in class so much the other kids say that I think I'm smarter than they are?

- **What if** I make straight A's and my best friend feels bad because she makes B's?

- **What if** I do my best performance in the talent show and some kids say I think I'm all that?

- **What if** I go all out on a project and everybody thinks I'm a geek?

Those "What Ifs" can make you feel like you're constantly holding yourself in until you're ready to explode. Before you do, here's "What IS":

- God gave you a wonderful mind so you can expand it, not shrink it!

- You have a job to do with that mind: to make a difference in the world. You can't make that difference if you pretend to be less than you are.

- There are always people who will be jealous of your talent or your courage to use it. Jealousy can make people say some pretty mean things so they don't have to feel guilty because they aren't using **their** gifts.

- Most people will be inspired by a brave, nothing-held-back performance. Do your thing to the limit and beyond, and you'll give other people the courage to do the same.

- What does "geek" mean anyway? The word is usually used by kids who don't understand how amazing it feels to really get into a thing, learn all about it, and share it with other people in an awesome way. Do you want to trade that feeling for their approval? Hey, don't cheat yourself by being a too-small version of the real you.

BOHO #4: Thinking you won't be able to "keep up" if you live honestly. You're always dodging questions like …

- **What if** I don't do a sport or an activity every day after school and I miss something (popularity, awards, everybody thinking I'm wonderful at everything)?

- **What if** I don't get the clothes my friends are wearing—even though I don't like them—and they don't want to be seen with me because I look stupid?

- **What if** I mess up on the test and don't get recommended for honors classes or the gifted program? And then I don't get into college? And then I can't get a job? And then I'm homeless ...

- **What if** I don't join in the gossiping—even though I hate talking about people behind their backs—and I don't get invited to the good sleepovers anymore?

The world can make you pretty crazy with all its expectations. But here's "What IS":

- Trying to do it all doesn't make you good at everything. In fact, it doesn't even let you be as good as you could be at **some** things, like the things you were **meant** to do.

- If the clothes you wear make the difference between whether your friends accept you or vote you out of the group, they seriously don't qualify as friends. There are other girls who will like you no matter where you shop.

- Those who are talented in academics (schoolwork) aren't the only ones with special gifts. Use the ones you have where you can. There's more than one way to be smart.

- Being a part of a group should never mean you have to go against what you know is right. You'll be much happier hanging out with people who have the same values you do.

- The surest way to fail is to try to match everything everybody else is doing.

- Find your own rhythm and walk to it. There is no "keeping up" on this journey to the real you.

Bottom line: No matter what people say—"She's just weird," or "She's so goody-goody, she's not any fun," or "She thinks she's all that"—almost everyone at least secretly likes the authentic person. Real, honest, genuine people are so attractive, only the most insecure don't at least admire them from afar. The more you are like yourself, the more easily you can allow others to be themselves, and just about everybody likes that feeling.

> I'm known as Little Miss Perfect. People think I don't take enough chances when it comes to getting in trouble and living off the hook. I don't see what's so wrong about doing good, but when I'm around them I feel stiff.

That Is SO Me!

Are you ready to apply all that to yourself? Then think about what it feels like when you *aren't* being the real you and you know it. Try to see a picture in your mind that matches that feeling. Here are some images your fellow mini-women have come up with:

"I think of a puppet, with somebody else pulling the strings."

"It's like I'm in a cave, looking out."

"I can almost feel myself getting smaller and smaller."
What's your mind-picture? _____

_____

Now draw that picture on paper. You may want to keep it with your journal and look at it every so often and write about times when you feel like that. Definitely, whenever you get that feeling, stop and say to yourself: *Oops. I'm not being the Unique Me. What needs to happen?*

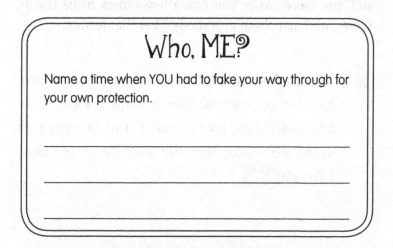

Who, ME?

Name a time when YOU had to fake your way through for your own protection.

_____

_____

_____

HERE'S THE DEAL ON WHEN YOU CAN FAKE IT

When you need to protect yourself:

There are certain situations where it's okay—and probably good!—to put a mask over your feelings as you're walking the journey. That's when showing how you really feel would only make things worse. Some examples from other mini-women will show you what I mean:

““Once I was babysitting, and the kids tied me up while we were playing cops and robbers. I was stuck and it scared me, like, to death, but I acted like it was all part of the game. That wasn't much fun for them, since I didn't scream my head off, so they untied me.””

““I was walking home from school, and these boys were following me and calling me names like Wide Load and Blubber. I really wanted to cry and scream at them to leave me alone, but I knew if I did that, they'd never stop. So I just held my head up and kept walking as if it didn't bother me. Then when I got inside my house, I cried for like an hour.””

““I get so scared before a dance performance that I just want to run away. But I know as soon as I get on stage and start dancing, I'm going to forget all about being nervous, so I just pretend I'm totally cool with it. That's the only way I can control the jitters.””

Just be sure to do two things when you "fake it 'til you make it":

1. Be honest with yourself about how you really feel. Trying to fake yourself out is never a good idea!

2. Make sure you have a chance to express your true feelings when it's safe to do that. Keeping them forever bottled up isn't a good plan either.

When it's fun!

Have you ever tried on different selves on purpose? Like when you're spending the night with friends and you give each other new hairstyles or dress up in costumes—how fun is that? It's actually part of finding out what feels real to you.

Ever get the urge to try out a sport or a different handwriting style or a new attitude ... just to see if it fits? That's one way to discover yourself too, as long as you're honest about what just *doesn't* feel like the Unique You.

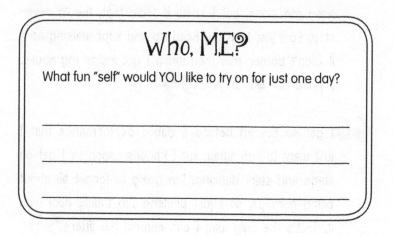

Who, ME?

What fun "self" would YOU like to try on for just one day?

_____

_____

_____

GOT GOD?

It's all sounding pretty great, isn't it? But there will still be times when it's just so hard to be true to yourself ...

- Times when your interests start to change and your friends stay the same.

- Or when a new trend starts that you don't like and you feel left out.

- Or when somebody is really going to be disappointed if you don't do it her way.

I could tell you to just "bite the bullet" and deal with it, but there's a better, kinder way, and that way is God.

Our heavenly Father gets how tough it can be, so you're not left to navigate through all this by yourself. The Bible is full of verses that tell you God is there for you even when nobody else is, but here's one where Jesus seems to be speaking just to mini-women:

> "You all have a single Teacher, and you are all classmates. Don't set people up as experts over your life, letting them tell you what to do. Save that authority for God; let *him* tell you what to do."
>
> Matthew 23:8–9 THE MESSAGE

Maybe you'll be "between friends" for a short time. Or you'll feel a little lonely until that new trend becomes so yesterday. Or you'll have to wait it out until someone's disappointment turns to "Oh, I get it now." But God will be there in that deep-down sense that you're doing it right. That you're being real. God doesn't promise you "easy." But God does promise love and peace. That's good stuff for the journey.

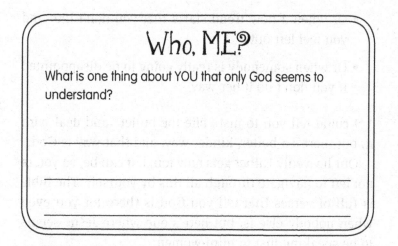

Who, ME?

What is one thing about YOU that only God seems to understand?

_____

_____

_____

That Is SO Me!

Let's check out your personal BOHOs.

STEP 1: Draw something hairy next to any of the following that push you to be somebody other than who you really are.

_____ my need to be perfect

_____ my desire to be cool

_____ what my friends think

_____ what the popular kids think

_____ what my siblings say

_____ what I see on TV or in movies or magazines

_____ things I don't want anybody to know about me

_____ my need to impress people

_____ my love of attention

_____ my fear that people will look at me

_____ the lies I tell so I won't feel like I'm weird

_____ my fear that my friends will dump me if I'm not the same as they are

_____ my fear of being left out

_____ feelings I don't want anybody to know I have

_____ other kids' teasing because I do really well in school

_____ my fear that I'm not good enough

_____ my fear that if I don't "keep up" I'll be left behind

In this empty space, draw or write anything else that's a BOHO for you.

STEP 2: Now number the BOHOs you've drawn a hairy image next to. Number 1 will be your biggest obstacle to always being yourself, and your last number will be the smallest obstacle. The blank ones aren't obstacles at all. Yay!

Just knowing what's blocking you—and how big it is to you—will help you to be aware of how much you hide the real you. It's the first step in getting that hairy thing out of the way.

STEP 3: Remember this: It's almost impossible to completely destroy the barriers that keep you from doing your natural thing. There will always be jealous kids, demanding parents, and siblings who tease you until you want to flush them down the toilet. Even your own secret fears will hang around in the back of your mind. But just because they're there doesn't mean you can't get past them. That's what the rest of this book is about. Meanwhile, keep this in mind:

> For I am convinced that ... [nothing] ... will be able to separate us from the love of God that is in Christ Jesus our Lord.
>
> Romans 8:38–39

Ya got that? Nothing.

❝I wrote a story and then I read it out loud to some kids I know. They were like, 'Oh, that's so stupid.' I gave up writing for a while because I got so discouraged.❞

YOU CAN DO IT

Remember how I said in chapter 1 that this journey wasn't just going to be a sightseeing tour? It's now time to get some of it on you, because the best way to convince yourself that being you is a great feeling is to *experience* that.

How to make it happen:

STEP 1: Start by thinking of one thing you like to do that (here's the important part) none of your friends is into—or that you've never told them about because you're afraid they'll go, "There's no way you really want to do that!" Maybe it's ...

- Listening to music that isn't exactly popular (like opera or swing band or Gregorian chant).

- Reading books that don't qualify as hip (like the classics or poetry).

- Pursuing an unusual hobby (like juggling or raising tropical fish or collecting buttons).

- Concocting something exotic in the kitchen (like macaroni with goat cheese).

- Going to a secret place (like the attic or the basement or a corner of your mind).

- Planting things (maybe petunias or zucchini or pumpkin seeds).

- Doing something artsy (like designing a whole wardrobe or experimenting with a camera or writing your own movie scripts).

Whatever it is, write it here:

_____

STEP 2: Now make an appointment with yourself to do that little thing. You may need to check your schedule and the family's. Once you know you can carve out that hour, write it here:

DAY _____ DATE_____

TIME _____ PLACE _____

STEP 3: Gather all your materials—art supplies, iPod, gardening tools—everything you'll need or want for this hour of pure you.

STEP 4: On your way to the kitchen or the reading chair or wherever you're headed, decide that just for this time, you're not going to think about what your friends would say or whether your brother will tease you or whether anybody would laugh at you if this got out on Facebook. Just decide.

STEP 5: Then simply enjoy doing this thing that is totally and uniquely yours. Dance, sing, paint, stir like nobody's watching, since hopefully nobody is. Savor every minute as if you were licking your favorite ice cream, because being yourself is a delicious experience.

STEP 6: If it turns out to be your kind of fun, schedule another hour for next week—or try something else that has YOU written all over it. Nobody said this journey was going to be totally easy, but nobody said that it couldn't sometimes be a blast!

That's What I'm Talkin' About!

Here are a few suggestions for things to write about, or draw in your journal, or just think over when the real you and God are hanging out ...

Spending an hour doing something that was totally me felt _____

_____

_____.

More things I'd like to try include _____

_____

_____.

One step I could take to get my hairiest obstacle out of my way would be _____

_____

_____.

It seems strange that I ever thought _____

_____

was a big old hairy obstacle because now _____

_____

_____.

4

Talkin' Trash—Talkin' Truth

So far on your journey to the real you, you've discovered some very cool things about your unique self *and* some of the things that can keep you from *being* that self. If it were easy to just say, "I know what the big old hairy obstacles are, and I'm not going to let them get in my way," this book could end right here!

Your fellow mini-women will tell you it *isn't* that easy.

❝ I KNOW I'm going to grow into myself, but I still feel self-conscious about being chubby and flat-chested. **❞**

❝ I worry so much that I'm gonna make a wrong decision, I get, like, paralyzed and don't do anything at all. **❞**

❝ In dance I think, 'I'm so inflexible,' even though I'm the most flexible person in my whole class. Why do I do that? **❞**

But y'know what? You can get rid of those obstacles if you follow some more Rules of the Road, and that's what these next two chapters are about. Here's another one ...

When you're on a road trip, you don't leave a trail of litter from your car window. (Let's hope not, anyway!) The same goes for the journey to the real you. If you toss around trash talk about yourself, you'll block out the beauty that's there. Let's look at those possible pieces of trash so you can put them in their proper place—in with the garbage!

Who, ME?

What's the first "I'm so _____"
that comes into YOUR mind?

Who, ME?

Turn YOUR "I'm _____"
into a treasure.

_____

Turn YOUR "I'm so _____"
into a compliment to someone else.

_____

Who, ME?

What "if only" could YOU use some help with?

_____

_____

_____

Who, ME?

What's the first thing that comes into YOUR mind when you think, "I can't _____"?

Who, ME?

What's one thing YOU have missed out on because you said, "I can't"?

_____

_____

_____

Who, ME?

What have YOU been afraid of that you could at least try?

_____

_____

_____

Who, ME?

Can YOU change your "if only," or do you need to accept it?

_____

_____

Who, ME?

What's the first "if only" that comes into YOUR mind?

_____

_____

HERE'S THE DEAL ABOUT TALKIN' TRASH

Three main "trash" phrases can litter the journey to the Unique You.

Piece of Trash #1—"I'm so _____."

Mini-women can fill in that blank with as many answers as there are tween girls themselves.

• *I'm so fat.*

• *I'm so totally dumb in math.*

• *I'm so spastic at sports.*

• *I SO have the biggest mouth in life.*

- *I'm so lame at art.*

- *I'm so much of a loser!*

You probably wouldn't say those things to your best friends. And since you now know that God wants you to love yourself just as you do your "neighbor," it only makes sense that you shouldn't say them to yourself either. That can be a hard habit to break, so try these side roads:

Route 1: Turn those pieces of trash into treasures.

- "I'm so fat" becomes "I'm gonna eat something healthy."

- "I'm dumb in math" becomes "I'll get a math tutor."

- "I'm so spastic at sports" becomes "It's fun to cheer people on."

- "I have the biggest mouth" becomes "I can talk to just about anybody."

- "I'm lame at art" becomes "I like to draw for fun."

- "I'm a loser" becomes "How can I be a total loser when everyone's a winner at something?"

Route 2: If you just can't say anything positive about yourself, say something positive about somebody else.

- Not "I'm so fat," but "She looks so cute in that outfit."

- Not "I'm dumb in math," but "You are, like, the class math whiz."

Route 3: Do NOT add an insult to yourself when you compliment someone else. "She looks so cute in that outfit. I wish I were skinny like her."

But DO add a request for help: "You are, like, the class math whiz. Could you help me with the homework?"

Hating anything about your true self makes you more false, not more real. If you hate it, you're going to try to cover it up and try to be something else. If you look at it as a challenge or just hug it, then you can keep going toward the Unique You.

Piece of Trash #2—"I can't _____."

That line can be filled in with things you haven't even tried very hard to do. We're talking about things like these from your fellow mini-women:

- *I can't go to a party where I don't know anybody.*

- *I can't talk in front of people.*

- *I can't learn to ... (swim, dance, ski, ice-skate, bake brownies, do a cartwheel, eat a lobster ...).*

- *I can't get along with my sister/brother.*

- *I can't go to school when my friends are mad at me.*

Everybody gets freaked out sometimes when there's something new to try—from going to a different school to eating sushi for the first time. Instead of wailing, "I can't!" try these alternate routes:

Route 4: Give it an honest effort. Sometimes we'll say we can't when what we really mean is, "I'm afraid I'll fail and look like an idiot, so I'm not even going to attempt it." You can miss out on a lot of cool stuff that way.

Route 5: If it turns out you really can't do it, you'll know you need some more help (like in a school subject or an important relationship), or you'll discover that it really isn't your thing (like in a sport or one of the arts).

Either way, you'll have the satisfaction of knowing you gave it a shot, and that can really build your confidence in yourself.

So instead of saying, "I can't," say, "I'll try." Like this...

- "I don't like going to parties where I don't know anybody, but I can try to make some new friends at this one."

- "I get shy talking in front of people, but I can try doing my report for just my family before I have to do it in class."

- "I don't know how to swim yet, but I'll try taking lessons."

- "My little brother drives me nuts, but I'm gonna try not to smack him for at least three days."

- "My friends at school are all mad at me, but I'm going to try to make up."

Piece of Trash #3—"If only _____."

We say "If only _____" when we think one change in us would make absolutely everything different.

- "If only I weren't bigger than everyone else in my whole entire class."

- "If only I were funnier."

- "If only I didn't get my feelings hurt so easy."

- "If only I were the best at something ... anything!"

In the first place, one thing being different won't make

life perfect. There are other routes to take, though, that can make it better.

Route 6: Before you say "if only," decide whether it's about something you can actually change or something you need to just accept.

You can't change...

- **your height or your nose or the shape of your face.** And why would you want to? That's what you look like, not who you are. When you want to look your best, do it so you'll feel beautiful inside and out, not so other people will like you.

- **the qualities you were born with.** You might not be funny, for example, but who says you have to be? Polish up your knack for encouraging people, or for getting them to talk about themselves, or for making them see they're about to do something stupid.

Route 7: Instead of saying, "If only," start saying, "I always."

- "I always try to look exactly like me."

- "I always give my friends the best of who I am (or at least I try to)."

- "I always try to see both sides before I decide that somebody meant to hurt my feelings."

- "I always look for ways to improve at the things I have to do and the things I love to do."

Who, ME?

How could your "if only" be an "I always"?

_____

_____

That Is SO Me!

It's time to check out your own "I'm so _____'s," "I can't _____'s" and "If only _____'s" so you can watch out for them in your thoughts and in your talk. It's so much easier to keep the trash out when you know what it is!

STEP 1: Circle every trash-talkin' area that gets hung up in your mind. There's a space to write in your own area if it's missing here.

What negative things do you say, "I'm so _____" about?

my height   my weight   my face

my hair   my schoolwork   my athletic ability

my artistic talent   how I get along with people

my popularity   my laugh   how I talk

how outgoing I am

Anything else? _____

What do you say "I can't _____" about?

sports   exercise   outdoor activities

subjects in school   how I organize my schoolwork

how I behave in school

how I get along with teachers

how I get along with other kids

how I get along with my family   chores

my appearance   artistic activities

Anything else? _____

What negative things do you say "If only _____" about?

money   material stuff   my room

my family   school subjects   teachers

the school day   sports   artistic activities

my hobbies   kids at school   friends

church   pets   my body

my appearance

Anything else? _____

STEP 2: Look at the areas of your life you've circled above. Make a list (in your journal would be a good place) of the exact things you tell yourself about each one.

Examples:

- popularity—"I'm so outside the cool kids' group."

- how I organize my schoolwork—"I can't ever find anything. I'm just a ditz."

- teachers—"If only I were smarter. Then Mrs. What's-Her-Name would like me."

STEP 3: Now you can sweep out each piece of trash and replace it with the truth ...

- "I'm cool enough to start my own group of friends."

- "I can get Mrs. What's-Her-Name to help me get organized—and while I'm at it, I can get help with math too."

GOT GOD?

You won't be able to snap your fingers and immediately become a truth-teller instead of a trash-spreader, especially when just about everyone you know goes around saying, "I am so—," "I can't—," and "If only—." You're going to need God's help, and here's one way to know it's there.

- Grab your Bible and read the story of the prodigal son in Luke 15:11–24. If you don't have a Bible, the gist of the parable is that a rich man's son asked for his inheritance from his father and went out and partied it away until he found himself living in a pigsty (for real). He decided to go back to his father and ask if he could be one of his slaves. But his father not only forgave him, but he also threw a party for him so he would know how much he was loved in spite of the, well, pretty stupid things he'd done.

- Imagine that you were that partying prodigal son returning to your father. How would you fill in the blanks?

  ‣ "I'm so _____."

  ‣ "I can't _____."

  ‣ "If only _____."

- The son didn't know the alternate routes you've just learned about, but his father did. He said …

  ‣ You messed up, but I understand (Verse 20)

  ‣ You've been lost, but now you're found (Verse 24).

  ‣ Let's celebrate your discovering real life (Verse 24).

- And who was the Father in the story who turned that trash into treasure? God, of course. So every time you think of speaking garbage about yourself, turn to the Father the way that son did, and …

  ‣ Know he's always there.

  ‣ Run to him. (Pray!)

  ‣ Ask for forgiveness and help.

  ‣ Believe that you are his beloved child—and that's all that matters.

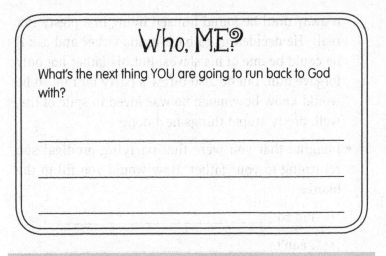

Who, ME?

What's the next thing YOU are going to run back to God with?

_____

_____

_____

YOU CAN DO IT

One of the best things you can do to stop thinking and talking trash about yourself is to be grateful for everything that's wonderful about you and your life. You can get a start on that by making and filling a **treasure chest**.

What you'll need:

○ A box—a shoebox is fine. If you want to really go all out, ask your mom if you can use that old toy box or an empty bin (the kind she stores the Christmas decorations in), but think about where you're going to keep it first.

○ Decorative items—Use anything you want to decorate it the way you imagine your perfect treasure chest ought to look. It doesn't have to become something out of _Pirates of the Caribbean_, as long as it looks like it belongs to you.

How to make it happen:

○ Decorate your box until it really says you.

○ Fill it with things that represent what's great about you and your life. Here are some ideas:

▸ pictures of you with friends and family, or shots of you that capture your special moods

▸ artwork you've done

▸ stories you've written

▸ souvenirs of your activities (last year's soccer cleats, dance recital programs, a piece from your shell colloection ...)

▸ notes and cards from people expressing their love for you

▸ reminders of special occasions

▸ anything that says something positive about you (your favorite flower pressec into your most-loved book, a miniature soccer ball, your name spelled out in sequins on paper ...)

○ Write a letter to yourself. Tell yourself everything you appreciate about you. Remind yourself of all the things you love about your life. Promise yourself you'll try never to put any of that down, or wish you were more, or had more. Decorate a copy of the letter to match yourself and keep that in your treasure chest too.

There's no room for trash when you know ...

- what a treasure your life is.
- how thankful you can be for just being who you are.
- what's really important to you.
- how important you are to God.

Ya gotta love that.
And from now on?

- Add to your treasure chest when you discover something new about yourself. It's going to happen a lot!

- Go to your treasure chest as often as you want, but especially when you find yourself having a bad case of the "If only's," the "I'm so's," or the "I can'ts." It will help you remember that's trash talk, and you'll soon be talking truth and treasure to yourself. After all, we are most ourselves when we love the most.

That's What I'm Talkin' About!

When you and God and your journal are chatting, these are some things you might want to consider:

Now I know the worst lie I *used* to believe about myself was _____

_____

_____.

One thing I'm learning to accept about myself is _____

_____

_____

_____.

One thing I *don't* want to change about myself is _____

_____

_____

_____.

The next new thing I'm going to try is _____

_____

_____

_____.

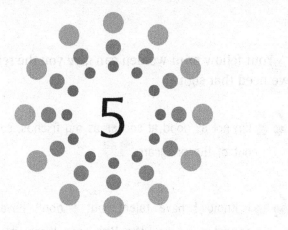

5

Being You—Being Her

Another Rule of the Road for this journey to the real you
is this one:

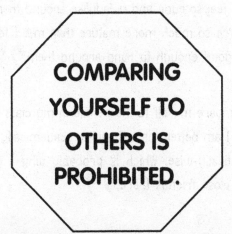

**COMPARING
YOURSELF TO
OTHERS IS
PROHIBITED.**

Your fellow mini-women can give you the reasons why we need that sign:

> 66 I'm not as good at soccer as my friends, so I dropped out of the program. 99

> 66 I know I have talent, but I don't have as many opportunities as Little Miss over there, so what's the point? 99

> 66 I beat myself up over my schoolwork a lot because the guys in my class always finish our homework assignments within like one day, yet I work on home-work almost CONSTANTLY just to get it done in THREE. It makes me feel stupid. 99

> 66 When I'm with my older sister and her friend, I some-how feel so rude and unladylike around them because they're so much more mature than me. I feel like I'm not good enough to hang around them. 99

> 66 I compare myself to the people in my class and I find that I am better maturity-wise, academically-wise, and artistically-wise. Which is probably why I don't have any close friends there. 99

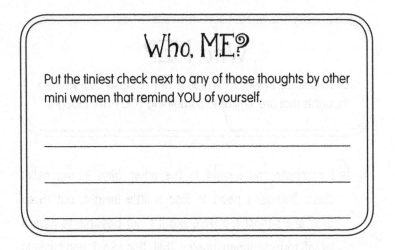

Who, ME?

Put the tiniest check next to any of those thoughts by other mini women that remind YOU of yourself.

_____

_____

_____

It's not sounding like anybody feels very real in those situations. In fact, going down the Comparison Dead End is one of the best ways to lose who YOU are because you're always measuring yourself against who everybody ELSE is.

So on this leg of the journey to the real you, what do you say we see that dead end for what it is and make a U-turn?

Who, ME?

Add YOUR comparison to that list of dead ends.

_____

_____

_____

Who, ME?

Draw a small frowny face next to any of those mini women thoughts that are similar to something YOU have thought.

66 I compare my weight to the other girls in my ballet class. I know I need to lose a little weight, but those girls are almost too thin, like it's not possible to have a lot of muscle when you're that thin. So I don't really want to be their size, but standing next to them in a leotard and tights makes me look even more over-weight than I am. **99**

Who, ME?

Have YOU dragged a friend into the comparison dead end lately?

_____

_____

How's that working out for you?

_____

> **"** Sometimes I'm not myself because my aunt brags and brags on her kids that are my age to EVERYBODY all the TIME! I feel like I do not measure up to them even if it is not 'quite' like my aunt says ... **"**

> **"** My friends and I are so competitive, we can't even look at our toes without comparing them! I cry almost every time I lose, and I think I just need to drop out of the constant competition and just be me. **"**

Who, ME?

Put one of those frowny faces next to any of those mini women questions YOU have asked yourself.

What is real about driving yourself nuts? Here's an alternate route for you:

> **"** I sometimes compare myself with other people. But that only makes me feel worse and bad about myself. So what's the point? Right? I mean, if I can't change myself about some things that God put in me, then why bother comparing? Some qualities of others might be good to have, such as being neat or always turning homework in on time, but I think we should never compare who we are to who other people are. **"**

HERE'S THE DEAL ABOUT THE COMPARISON DEAD END

Most of the time when we hold ourselves up against other people, we come out with things like these confessions from mini-women:

- "I notice strangers at the store and think they have prettier hair than me."

- "I can't draw like the other kids do."

- "I can't dance as well as the best girls in my ballet class."

- "I'm a little mathematical point next to my sister who can do everything right."

As one tween girl put it so well:

"I compare myself to other people and always end up worse—the underdog."

That's bad enough. But the further we go into that dead end, the more likely we are to think things like:

- I might not be all that smart, but at least I'm not a stuck-up snob about my grades like she is.

- I may not be as cute, but I think I'm way nicer.

- Who wants to be popular anyway? She just thinks she's all that.

Once again, a girl who is right where you are put it best:

"I compare myself with others a lot, and it's hard to admit, but PRIDE and JEALOUSY are kinda top in my vocab. It's horrible, I know, because often it ends up in a bad attitude from me to the other person who has no idea what's going on."

If you slip around the final bend into the Comparison Dead End, you'll hear yourself saying things like, "I heard that she makes A's by cheating. I think I might have even seen her do it."

By the time you get to that point, you're so far away from yourself, you can't find your way back. How does that happen?

1. You focus so much on what you **aren't**, you don't think about what you **are**. Just you. Not you compared to everybody else.

2. It's hard to live with thinking you're less than other people, so you find ways to bring them down with you. Since that isn't the way you really want to act, you aren't being yourself.

3. But when you don't feel better, you have to bring your friends into it with you. Maybe you'll feel less "inferior" if you can make that "superior" person miserable. It doesn't work, though, because deep inside you really hate what you're doing, which is becoming something you're not.

So how do you stop doing that? It isn't easy, because the world we live in measures people against each other all the time.

- The Olympics compares athletes to see who's the best in the world.

- Every sport has its version of the Super Bowl to see who the champions are.

- Beauty pageants determine who's the prettiest.

- You probably know who the smartest kid in your class is. And the most athletic. And the most artistic. That's because "the best" always get recognized.

Okay, so some competition can be fun and challenge people to do their very best. But it isn't meant to tell people whether they're better or worse than somebody else as people. And it SURE isn't something *you* need to do in everyday situations. Seriously, what is the *point* of asking yourself these questions:

- Do my parents love me more than they do my siblings?

- Am I smarter or dumber than the rest of my class?

- Is my artwork the best of anybody I know?

- Do I get as much attention in class as my best friend?

- Do I get invited to as many parties as the "cool girls"?

- Do I dance better than the rest of the girls in my studio?

- Am I a better athlete than any girl who has ever gone before me?

Route 8: Instead of asking those questions, ask yourself, "Does it matter?" Really. Does it matter whether you're smarter, more talented, more popular, or more loved than anybody else on the planet?

Uh, no. What **matters** is that ...

- You are as loving to your family as YOU can be.

- You do YOUR best in school.

- You develop your talents the best YOU can.

- You treat other people the way YOU want to be treated.

- You ask for help when YOU need it.

- You keep trying when YOU make a mistake.

Here's another alternate route to help you avoid the Comparison Dead End.

Route 9: Only compare yourself to the person you were yesterday. Are you just a little more real today? That means you're making progress on YOUR journey.

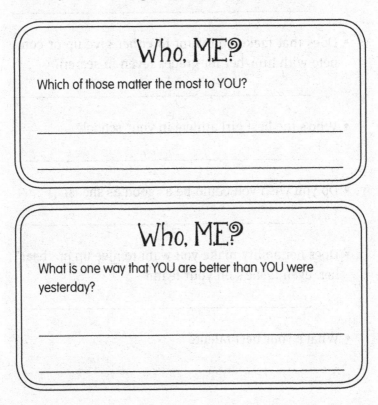

Who, ME?

Which of those matter the most to YOU?

_____

_____

Who, ME?

What is one way that YOU are better than YOU were yesterday?

_____

_____

That Is SO Me!

Let's find out who you might be comparing yourself to. Answer each of these questions honestly, of course. You can write *no*, *nobody*, or *I don't know* if that's your true answer.

- Who's the smartest kid in your class?

  _____

- Do you think you're smarter or "dumber" than him/her?

  _____

- Does that make you want to either give up or compete with him/her for grades (even in secret)?

  _____

- Who's the best girl athlete in your school?

  _____

- Do you wish you could be as good as she is?

  _____

- Does her ability make you want to give up or "beat" her, even if she's on your team?

  _____

- What's your best talent?

  _____

- Do you know somebody your age who you think is more talented than you are at your best talent?

  _____

- Does her talent make you want to either give up or take her place from her?

  _____

- Who's the most popular girl you know?

  _____

- Do you think she's more likable than you are?

  _____

- Does her popularity make you feel like a nobody or like taking her title as Miss Popularity?

  _____

- Who do you think is your teacher's "pet"?

  _____

- Does seeing her do her "pet" thing make you want to either misbehave or steal her position?

  _____

Look over your answers. If you have any NOs, *nobodys*, or *I don't knows*, good for you. You don't always take the Comparison Dead End, and from now on you'll probably go there less and less. Wherever you don't have NO or *nobody* or *I don't know*, think about what you've reported and have a big ol' belly laugh. Really. WHAT were you thinking, huh? Give yourself a break from figuring out where you stand next to everyone else. That's way less fun than just being the best you can be.

Who, ME?

"The people I know accept me for who I am and don't try to be better than me or try to treat me like an outsider."

• •

GOT GOD?

There's also more to it than feeling better about yourself. The Comparison Dead End can keep you away from important truths about your life. Truths that come from God. Here's one biggie.

> For you [God] created my inmost being;
> you knit me together in my mother's womb.
> I praise you because I am fearfully and wonderfully made;
> your works are wonderful,
> I know that full well.
> My frame was not hidden from you
> when I was made in the secret place,
> when I was woven together in the depths of the earth.
> Your eyes saw my unformed body;
> all the days ordained for me were written in your book
> before one of them came to be.

Psalm 139:13–16

It's pretty clear that you were custom-designed. Tailor-made. Handcrafted. Set up for a purpose nobody else has.

So doesn't it make sense—if God has a unique, one-of-a-kind plan for your life, which he decided before he even started making you—that he gave you the right personality to carry it out? That personality is different from everyone else's because each person has a unique plan. Contrary to what you hear, there is no "model person" everybody is supposed to copy.

Oh, and about that plan ...

> "For I know the plans I have for you," declares the Lord, "plans to prosper you and not to harm you, plans to give you hope and a future."
>
> Jeremiah 29:11

Why miss out on what God has in store for you while you're trying to get in on his plan for somebody else? Your plans are the best—for YOU!

The same goes for comparing yourself to other people and deciding you're BETTER than they are! You know, "I'm not as pretty, but I'm WAY smarter."

Jesus taught us about that in the story about the Pharisee who prayed, "God, I thank you that I am not like other people" (Luke 18:11). If, like the Pharisee, you go around with your nose in the air, you might end up falling flat on your face. Be content with who you are, Jesus tells us—no more, no less. After all, God thought the real you was worth dying for.

● ●

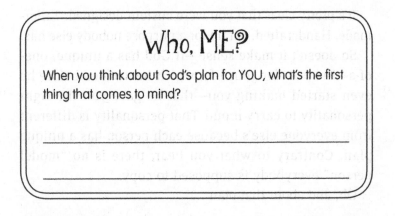

Who, ME?

When you think about God's plan for YOU, what's the first thing that comes to mind?

_____

_____

That Is SO Me!

One sure way to avoid getting trapped in the Comparison Dead End is to have so much fun being YOU, it seems absolutely ridiculous to wonder what it's like to be somebody else. Try this quiz just for giggles. It's even more of a riot when you do it with friends. It's good sleepover material.

Choose one of the answers in each category that best fits your real self or write your own idea in the space provided.

- If I were a car, I'd be a

_____ cherry-red sports car

_____ yellow pickup truck

_____ silver luxury sedan

_____ white SUV

other: _____

- If I were a dog, I'd be a

    _____ golden retriever

    _____ miniature poodle

    _____ Doberman pinscher

    _____ beagle

    other: _____

- If I were a color, I'd be

    _____ shocking pink

    _____ candy-apple red

    _____ sunshine yellow

    _____ frog green

    _____ M&M blue

    other: _____

- If I were a song, I'd be

    _____ rock

    _____ country

    _____ rap

    _____ opera

    other: _____

- If I were a restaurant, I'd be a

  _____ a fast-food burger stop

  _____ a fine dining room with tablecloths

  _____ a health-food café

  _____ a sushi bar

  _____ other:

- If I were a couch, I'd be

  _____ genuine leather

  _____ a sectional with tons of pillows

  _____ white microfiber

  _____ Victorian

  _____ other:

- If I were a vacation, I'd be

  _____ a hike in the Rockies

  _____ a cruise in the Caribbean

  _____ a week in a theme park

  _____ a sightseeing tour in Europe

  _____ other:

Now put them all together and see if what you've chosen describes the real you. Here's an example:

I'm as practical and dependable as an SUV. I'm the beagle who gets the job done but who loves to play. I'm true blue, like the chorus to my favorite country song, like my favorite burger joint. You can lean on me like a comfy sofa and trust me because I'm a familiar walk in the woods. That's me, Molly Ann McPherson. Nice to meet you.

You don't have to write yours out if you don't want to, but do share it with the people who know you well—and who usually don't tell you who to be! Challenge them to take the quiz too. How fun to discover why the poodle in you doesn't always get along with the Doberman in your brother! And how you and your best friend can double the fun together because she's Disneyland and you're a hike in the Rockies!

HERE'S THE DEAL ABOUT ROLE MODELS

Now that you're seeing how much fun it is to be yourself, it's safe for you to look at the difference between wanting to BE other people and wanting to be LIKE them in some way.

Let's say there's an older girl, perhaps a friend of your big sister. You really admire her. Maybe you like the way she talks to you, like you're one of the girls instead of an annoying little pest. And maybe you've noticed how she's always ready to try something new, even your mom's brussels sprouts casserole. She can be honest but not hurt people's feelings, and you want to be like her someday.

That doesn't mean you want to trade yourself in for a carbon copy of that girl. It does mean ...

- She behaves in a way that appeals to you.

- There is nothing wrong with wanting to act that way too.

- In fact, it's right because what you admire in her is what God wants to see in all of us: kindness, confidence, and honesty.

Think about one person you look up to and respect, even among kids your own age. What is it about her (or him) that makes you think she (or he) is awesome? Could it be that ...

- She doesn't get mad easily.

- She treats every person like that person is worth a lot.

- She seems happy with what she has.

- She doesn't brag.

- She is always sharing with people.

- She encourages everyone.

- She makes people smile instead of frown.

- She feels sad when something bad happens to someone else, even someone she's not friends with.

- She celebrates with people instead of being jealous of them.

- She stands up for her friends.

- She is a person people can trust.

- She keeps a positive attitude instead of whining.

- She doesn't give up easily.

She might be quiet or the class clown but still has those qualities. She might be a soccer player or a bookworm and be like that just the same. It's not about her personality or her clothes or the awards she has hanging up in her room. It's about the way she loves people. And it's a good thing to want to love the way she does. In fact, that's the one way God wants all of us to be the same.

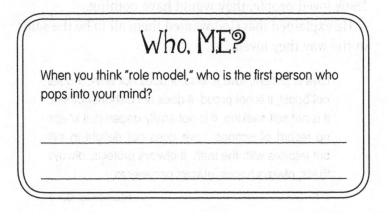

Who, ME?

When you think "role model," who is the first person who pops into your mind?

_____

_____

● ●

GOT GOD?

Evidently the people in a town called Corinth, back in the early days of Christianity, were trapped in the Comparison Dead End. They argued about everything ...

- Who was the best at speaking in tongues?

- Why did this guy have the gift of prophecy and this other guy didn't?

- That lady could heal a sick person with her faith, but that one, now, she could move mountains.

- One person sold half of what he owned for the poor, so the next guy sold *everything* ...

It was a mess, so Paul wrote a letter telling them to get out of that dead end. They all had certain gifts, and they ought to be using them for the good of the whole community. He said it didn't matter how they used their talents because if they didn't ALL start loving each other the way Jesus loved people, they would have nothing.

He explained that God wanted them all to be the same in the way they loved.

> Love is patient, love is kind. It does not envy, it does not boast, it is not proud. It does not dishonor others, it is not self-seeking, it is not easily angered, it keeps no record of wrongs. Love does not delight in evil but rejoices with the truth. It always protects, always trusts, always hopes, always perseveres.

> 1 Corinthians 13:4–7

When you discover someone who loves that way, that person can be a **role model** for you. By watching that person, you can learn how to express love like that too. You aren't copying her. You're being influenced by her.

This is looking to someone as a role model: Your teacher says something positive to every student coming into the room every morning. You do the same thing with the people who sit around you. Then you start doing it at home at breakfast.

This is trying to BE someone else: Your best friend has a funny, snorty laugh that everybody likes. You practice for hours trying to laugh the same way.

This is looking to someone as a role model: The cool teenage girl who babysits for you and your siblings never yells at your little brother, who has been known to bring past babysitters to tears. She plays Superman with him, calls him "Pal," and smiles at him a lot. You decide to be nicer to him instead of screaming at him every time he comes into your room.

This is trying to BE someone else: The girl everybody seems to like tells jokes at lunch every day. You memorize a bunch to share at the table and begin to tell one as soon as she sits down.

It's like Paul says:

> There are different kinds of gifts, but the same Spirit distributes them.
>
> 1 Corinthians 12:4

● ●

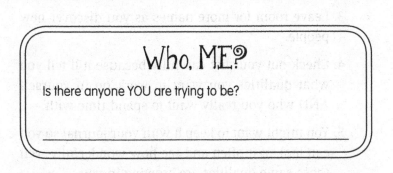

Who, ME?

Is there anyone YOU are trying to be?

_____

YOU CAN DO IT

For the next leg of our journey, it will help to make an **admiration list**, giving the names of people you know who have the qualities we talked about in "Got God?"

What you'll need:

○ a piece of the very coolest paper you can find

○ your favorite pens and markers

○ stickers, glitter, stencils for decorating your list (optional)

How to make it happen:

1. Write the names of all the people you admire who love the way God wants us to love (even though all their personalities may be different).

2. Decorate the list however you want to.

3. Leave room for more names as you discover new people.

4. Check out your list carefully because it'll tell you what qualities you want to work on in yourself AND who you really want to spend time with.

5. You might want to keep it with your journal so you can look at it often and see how wonderfully well those same qualities are growing in you.

6. Then you can love your true self even more.

That's What I'm Talkin' About!

You know the drill by now: Let these open-enders start off a discussion with God in your journal or just in your mind. Draw, doodle, or write 'til you drop!

When I finished my admiration list, I discovered that the person I admire most in this whole world is _____

_____

_____.

That says this about me: _____

_____

_____.

One person I've been comparing myself to who isn't such a good role model is _____

_____

_____.

One question I need to stop asking myself is: Am I as ___

_____

as _____

_____?

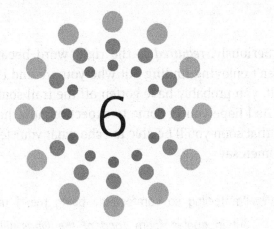

6

The Fun Part!

If the journey to the real you was *all* work and big hairy obstacles and rules, nobody would stick with it for long. So here's the Rule of the Road that keeps people traveling toward who they really are:

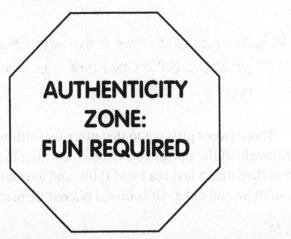

AUTHENTICITY ZONE: FUN REQUIRED

Seriously, *required* is the right word because if you aren't enjoying finding out who you are and being yourself, you probably have gotten off the trail somehow.

As I hope you've come to expect by now, help is here, so that soon you'll be able to echo what your fellow mini-women say:

> I'm feeling so comfortable being me, I might break out in quotes from *Lord of the Rings* with my best friend!

> I'm ready to restart my goal of reading through the Bible in a year. I think I can do it this time because I'm not worried about people saying I'm a Jesus freak. Like that's a bad thing anyway, right?

> Since I started to get to know myself better, I have this huge desire to redecorate my room.

> I'm ready to announce to my parents that I am not just a 'girly-girl' like they think. I just enjoy the finer things in life!

Those tween girls got to that place by working with me through all the things you've been learning in this book. But they didn't just read and think and journal. They got out there and did it. Of course, I offered them some travel guides, and now I'm offering them to you. If you're ready for this final leg together, get ready to do it too.

Who, ME?

What is the last totally fun thing YOU did by yourself?

_____

_____

Who, ME?

What tiny thing could you do to be better tomorrow than you are today?

_____

_____

Who, ME?

Name one tiny new thing YOU can try today.

_____

_____

HERE'S THE DEAL ABOUT ENJOYING BEING YOU

Travel Guide #1—Accept yourself each day. But don't settle for just staying as you are today. If it's in your power, be just a little better tomorrow.

- *I'm not naturally good at math, but if I spent fifteen minutes more on my homework every night, I could probably improve my grade.*

- *I'm shy, just like my mom, but if I asked that one girl about her horse, I bet she'd talk to me. It would even be okay if my face turned all red.*

Working at just an inch of improvement is way more fun that beating yourself up for not being who you want to be.

Travel Guide #2—Try one new thing every day. It doesn't have to be big or scary. Just new.

- *I'll say hi to that girl at school I've never spoken to before.*

- *I'm going to use one of our vocabulary words today and see if anybody notices.*

- *I think I'll try pickles on my peanut butter sandwich instead of jelly.*

- *Here goes—two cartwheels in a row instead of just one.*

Before you know it, all those small things will add up to a pretty big revelation of You!

Travel Guide #3—Let go of things that don't "fit" anymore. If it's not you, move on to something else.

- *I'm sick of reading fashion magazines ALL the time. I'm only keeping one of the hundred in my collection and throwing the rest away. Now I'm looking for better things to read, like craft mags.*

- *I'm sick of being on the soccer team just because my friends are when I pretty much stink at it. I'm starting a hiking club with my dad. That's way more me.*

- *I'm sick of having a messy room all the time. Instead of saying that's just the way I am (since I was like six), I'm having fun finding baskets and bins for everything and decorating them. I'm discovering I'm not just a natural slob.*

Travel Guide #4—Refuse to let small setbacks make you afraid to keep going.

- *I didn't get a part in the big church musical, but I'm gonna take drama at school this year and try again in the spring because I really like acting.*

- *I bruised my knee big-time when I fell on my skates, but I know what I did wrong. I totally love skating, so I'm ready to go for it again.*

- *I really think God wants me to be a writer, so even though my sister says my stories aren't that good, I'm going to keep practicing. It's like I can't NOT write!*

Just because you aren't spectacular at something doesn't mean you can't enjoy it. If you do, then it's you.

Travel Guide #5—If something totally draws your interest, learn all you can about it and give it a go.

- *I've always danced, but now I want to try singing and acting too. This year I'm taking choir AND joining drama club.*

- *I started going to auctions with my dad, and I totally love it. He's teaching me how to bid, and I'm saving up for something very cool.*

- *I found an old camera in our attic, and it still works, so I'm getting into photography. My grandpa says I have a good eye for picture-taking. Who knew?*

The world is filled with interesting stuff that goes way beyond iPhones and Facebook and even the select soccer team. Going after that interesting stuff makes for a more interesting you.

With those travel guides "packed," you're ready to continue the journey. And who better to provide directions than God himself?

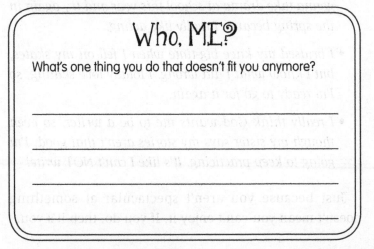

Who, ME?

What's one thing you do that doesn't fit you anymore?

_____

_____

_____

_____

Who, ME?

Name one small setback that has made you think less of yourself. Can you try again?

_____

_____

Who, ME?

Name one thing you're itching to learn more about.

_____

_____

• •

GOT GOD?

Some people think of the Bible as a book of rules, but it's more a collection of stories that *show* us rather than *tell* us how to live. The tales of people who were truly themselves can be super helpful as you go forward with the journey to the real you. Your fellow mini-women have pointed out several of their favorites for you:

I think I'll just let the mini-women speak for all of us on this one.

66 Esther was probably just about fifteen or sixteen, maybe even younger. But she wasn't afraid to be her true self and speak up, even though it might have gotten her killed. 99

66 David helps me, because he didn't let anyone really get to him when they teased him about being too young. 99

66 Mary could have been stoned to death for getting pregnant before she was married, but she believed in God's plan for her. She was only about fifteen. 99

66 Ruth was just being herself when she ignored Naomi telling her to go home. She went with her. It shows that it takes a lot of courage to be true to yourself. 99

66 Joseph's brothers hated him, but he never gave up on what he was supposed to do. It makes me have faith that God has an individual plan for me too. 99

66 Even though Paul and Silas were locked up and had every right to be sad and groan, whine, and ask God, 'Why me?' they sang and praised God because they were doing what they were meant to do. It reminds me not to whine about stuff about me that I can't change. 99

> **"** When Saul was on the way to Damascus to kill Christians, God gave him a different path, one that fit him better. So even when I'm on the wrong path, God will straighten me out! **"**

Who, ME?

What Bible story inspires YOU to be who YOU are no matter what?

_____

_____

That Is SO Me!

There are different "travel styles" for this part of your journey. Want to find out what yours is? Read the three approaches to the following situation and decide which one sounds MOST like you. Then read what that might say about you. Remember, each one is a great approach, so there is no right or wrong. There is just you!

Situation:

A few days before you start middle school, there's an activity fair in the gym. All the various clubs and sports have booths where you can talk to members and advisers and get a taste of what's available so you'll know what you might want to participate in. You can visit as many as you want, and there is only one rule: you have to be on your own; no going through the fair with your BFF like you're attached by Velcro. The gym doors open and—ready, set, go...

Approaches:

› A. You go from booth to booth in an orderly fashion, starting close to the door and working your way up and down the rows. If something looks kind of disorganized or the people in the booth are all over the place, you pass that one up. If an activity interests you and it seems like it's well run, you take their information sheet to study later.

› B. You walk along until you see a booth where the people are smiling and friendly and maybe even waving you over to them. If you feel good about what they tell you, you take their information sheet, even if it never occurred to you to join that kind of club before. What wouldn't be fun if you're with people you enjoy?

› C. You know you're looking for activities that challenge you, so you check out the ones that have interesting signs, lots of cool stuff, and people who aren't trying to see how many kids they can get to sign up. You ask a lot of questions, study the information sheets, and usually say you're going to think about it.

- D. You feel like you just walked into a huge banquet and everything looks delicious! Who knew there could be this much fun stuff to do? You flit among the very coolest booths and take every info sheet and sign up for a lot of things right on the spot, especially the ones where the people are like, "Come be in our club!" Be in it? You're practically ready to run it!

Your travel style:

If you chose (A), you travel with caution. It's not that you're a wimp or anything. You just like to know what's expected and who's in charge. Whether you play sports or join clubs or work to be in the Junior National Honor Society, you approach with care. If everything is hectic and confusing, forget about it.

If you chose (B), you love to go with what feels good. It's not that you can't think things through. You just don't usually have to because you have such good intuition. You especially enjoy activities that involve people you like, although if it's something you're drawn to and no one you know is a member, you'll make friends fast. If there's going to be a lot of fierce competition and drama, that's not for you.

If you chose (C), your journey includes a lot of thinking and planning. It isn't that you can't be fun. But fun for you is about being thoughtful and intelligent. It's about being mentally challenged, thinking things through, gathering the facts. If other people are on board with inventive projects, great. Those are your kind of people. If nobody wants to take the thing seriously, you'll move on. No big deal.

If you chose (D), you make fun just about every step of the way. It isn't that you don't get the meaning of things, but why can't important things be a complete blast too? As long as you can get out there and just do it, go for it full speed ahead, you're in heaven. The more creative, lively, even bizarre, the better as far as you're concerned. If people get too bogged down in rules and results, though, you have no problem picking—or inventing!—something else to do.

Whatever your true style is, embrace it like a big ol' teddy bear because that's the way you're sure to find You kind of things to do. Life pretty much is an activity fair, so approach it in style—your God-made style!

YOU CAN DO IT

Wouldn't it be so cool to make a **sound track** for your life right now? You know, a CD of songs that ...

- remind you of important times.

- put you in an accepting state of mind (open, eager, excited, hopeful).

- help you feel like yourslef.

- help you dream.

- inspire you to be your best self.

What you'll need:

- songs that fit the description above (copied from CDs or legally downloaded from the Internet)

- a blank CD and a CD burner or a program like iTunes on your computer where you can make a playlist

How to make it happen:

1. Listen to lots of music and choose your favorites.

2. Decide what order you want your songs to play in.

3. Rip or download each song, arrange them in a playlist, and (if you have the right stuff) burn that playlist onto a CD.

4. Decide on a name for your sound track and either make a label or type that name for your playlist.

5. Listen to your tape when you are …

   ‣ doing your homework

   ‣ writing in your journal

   ‣ falling asleep

   ‣ feeling down

   ‣ feeling confused

   ‣ trying to make a decision or solve a problem

   ‣ needing to remember who you really are

6. You can add to it whenever you discover a new "life song."

7. You can even start a new sound track on every birthday!

8. If you've made a CD, you can keep it in that treasure chest of yours.

That's What I'm Talkin' About!

In case your music inspires you to write in your journal or just have a quiet talk with God, here are some places you can go.

If I didn't know myself and I listened to my sound track, I would describe myself as _____

_____.

If I could design my own activity fair, I would have booths for _____

_____.

It's fun to be me because _____

_____.

The hard work of being myself is worth it because _____

_____.

7

Mileage Check

The journey to your true self is never over, which is great. I mean, now that you know what it's all about, would you *want* the adventure to end? One of your fellow mini-women says it perfectly:

> Now when I start comparing or feeling all awkward, I just remember that God made me unique, and that he loves me no matter what. That makes me just want to be MORE who I am instead of who other people think I'm supposed to be.

There is, however, one more Rule of the Road that I hope you'll pay attention to as you continue your journey—and that is:

It's sort of like consulting the map to make sure you're still on the right highway or seeing if another road might take you there—to the real you—faster. On our last leg of the journey together, let's see what the checkpoints are before you continue on.

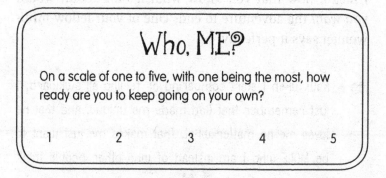

Who, ME?

On a scale of one to five, with one being the most, how ready are you to keep going on your own?

| 1 | 2 | 3 | 4 | 5 |

That Is SO Me!

The first checkpoint is a mileage check. Every so often, you'll just want to see how far you've come. You can do that right now.

Next to each of the issues below that you've been reading about in this book, write the number of "miles" you think you've "traveled."

- 3—I've come WAY far on that (or I was pretty close to start with).

- 2—I still have a ways to go, but I'm trying.

- 1—I haven't actually gotten started yet, but I'm ready now.

_____ avoiding attacks of the "Who Am I's?"

_____ loving myself

_____ accepting the things I can't change about myself

_____ showing other people who I really am

_____ discovering new things about myself

_____ not thinking I have to be perfect

_____ not trying to keep up with everyone else

_____ not trying to fit in (in ways that aren't me)

_____ spending some time doing things only I like to do

_____ being nice to myself

_____ not comparing myself to other people

_____ loving people the way God wants all of us to

_____ having fun being me

_____ doing what I know is right no matter what

Now add up your "miles." You'll come out with a number between 15 and 45, which you can write here:

_____

If you've traveled between 45 and 34 "miles," you're on a roll. Keep doing what you're doing and pay careful attention to the areas where you gave yourself less than a 3. Enjoy knowing that you're living a pretty authentic life and that it's only going to get better.

If you've come between 33 and 22 "miles," you have some you-work to do, but you're headed in the right direction. Look at the areas where you gave yourself a 1, and try to watch what's happening there. Even the smallest move will eventually get you there. Meanwhile, smile, because you're becoming the real you.

If the journey has brought you 21 to 15 "miles," you're just getting started, but there's nothing wrong with that. You have some fun challenges ahead. Just pick one area where you gave yourself a 1 and work on that until you feel pretty comfortable. Then work on another 1. Soon you'll discover that your miles have increased on things you hadn't even worked on. Yeah, baby. You're doin' it!

&& Now that I'm convinced God made me special, I don't usually judge people anymore. **"**

Who, ME?

Is the fact that you will never be expected to be "done" a relief to you—or a bummer?

_____

&& I got tired of having self-pity. Now I just say, 'I am fearfully and wonderfully made.' **"**

Who, ME?

What was the last wrong turn you took?

_____

_____

_____

HERE'S THE DEAL FOR THE REST OF THE JOURNEY

No matter where you are in the Unique You adventure right now, there are three things to remember as you continue on—things you'll want to check from time to time so the trip will go SO much smoother:

#1—Becoming who you really are takes your whole life. None of us is completely authentic until we're united with God in heaven. Life is all about the journey itself, and you'll enjoy it more as you grow closer to your true self. Try your best, but never expect to be "done."

#2—You'll change in a lot of ways as you continue to grow up. The idea is to be as real as you can be at any point on your journey. It'll be so cool to look back from time to time at how far you've come. (That's one of the best reasons for keeping a journal!) And always, deep inside, there will always be the real you that you were born to be.

#3—You're going to take turns that weren't meant for you. You might spend weeks, months, even years heading down some "street" that isn't yours. God will lead you back to the right one as long as you stay in touch with him. As soon as he does, put it behind you and move on. You have too much ahead to get stuck in shoulda, woulda, or coulda.

Remember those things, and you'll be all right, girl. You always will be.

GOT GOD?

Check out this verse. Think about it a little before you go on.

> "What about you?" [Jesus] asked. "Who do you say I am?"
>
> Simon Peter answered, "You are the Messiah, the Son of the living God."
>
> Jesus replied, "Blessed are you, Simon ... for this was not revealed to you by flesh and blood, but by my Father in heaven. And I tell you that you are Peter, and on this rock I will build my church."
>
> Matthew 16:15–18

Peter saw that Jesus really was the Son of God. As soon as Peter realized that and believed it, Jesus told Peter who **he** (Peter) was and what he (Jesus) wanted Peter to do.

It's the same for you. The more you discover that Jesus really is your teacher and your guide and your savior—and every other really good thing you can think of—the more clearly he will show you who **you** are and what he wants **you** to do.

So as you continue on the journey to the real you, anytime you feel lost or confused or just not sure, turn to him and tell him you know who he is. Then pay attention by doing the things we've talked about in this book. Somehow, he'll show you to yourself. Somehow, you will know.

Who, ME?

If Jesus asked you, "Who do you say I am?" what would you say in your own words?

_____

_____

_____

YOU CAN DO IT

It's time to give yourself a **bon voyage party**. You're setting out on an incredible journey, and that calls for a celebration just for you. Here are some celebration ideas, but you are always free to come up with something that is, of course, Uniquely You!

○ Give yourself a tea party.

○ Take yourself on a backyard picnic.

○ Have breakfast in bed.

○ Join yourself in an evening of dancing.

○ Treat yourself to a music festival with your ipod.

○ Invite yourself to an art exhibit of your best work.

○ Dribble your basketball (or bat softballs or kick your soccer ball) until you drop.

○ Make up a cheer about yourself.

○ Build the perfect-for-you ice-cream sundae (or pizza or sandwich or giant cookie).

○ Toast yourself with a glass of your favorite drink.

One more thing. Be sure to invite God to your celebration. He'll be there. He's been waiting for this all your life.

That's What I'm Talkin' About!

I hope you'll keep up with your journal and your treasure chest and all the other things you've started as we've journeyed through this book. For your last check-in before you take off on your own, you might want to discuss these things with God:

One way I feel different about myself now than when I started this book is _____

_____.

One thing I'm definitely going to keep doing now for the journey is _____

_____.

One Rule of the Road that will be kind of tough for me to follow is _____

_____.

The Rule of the Road or alternate Route or Travel Guide that's going to help me the most is _____

_____

_____.

Godspeed, mini-women!

the beauty of believing

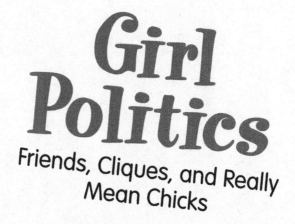

Girl Politics

Friends, Cliques, and Really Mean Chicks

REVISED EDITION

Nancy
Rue

ZONDERVAN®

ZONDERVAN.com/
AUTHORTRACKER
follow your favorite authors

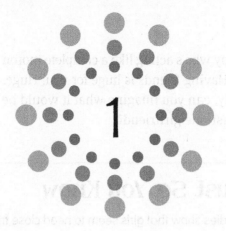

Why Can't We All Just Get Along?

You are a mini-woman.

That means you're no longer that sweet little baby girl-friend who plays with the other baby girlfriends her mom picks out and doesn't care who they are as long as they don't take the red crayon when she's using it.

It also means you haven't yet lost your mind and become a teenager who might ditch her BFF for the same guy you both thought was an annoying boy creature back when you were twelve—when you were mini-women, and therefore sane.

You are a mini-woman, which means you *get* that girl-friends are more important than the picture you're coloring or the boy who's acting like a complete moron to get your attention. Having friends is huge for you. Huge.

Seriously, can you imagine what it would be like not to have at least one girlfriend?

Just So You Know

Studies show that girls seem to need close friendships more than boys do.

What would you *do*—

- at lunchtime?

- at recess (because who plays on the swings anymore)?

- when something freaky happened to you?

- when something incredibly cool happened to you?

- when you were bored out of your skull?

- when your feelings were hurt and you ran to the bathroom crying?

- when you needed to know that very minute you were okay just like you are?

And how would you *feel* if you didn't have at least one friend?

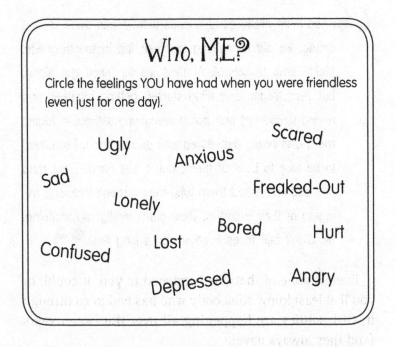

Who, ME?

Circle the feelings YOU have had when you were friendless (even just for one day).

Ugly

Scared

Anxious

Sad

Freaked-Out

Lonely

Bored

Hurt

Confused

Lost

Depressed

Angry

Whether you can't even imagine it or you're living it right now (ugh), it's not a news flash to you that having friends is mega-important.

It's just that it's not always easy.

No matter how much you love your BFF or your CFFs (that's Close Friends Forever), sometimes you're just not going to get along. (Ya think?)

You *can* make up and go, "What were we even fighting about?" … but sometimes you don't.

Girls who don't even *like* you can get involved.

A girl, or a whole group of girls, can decide that making you miserable is their new career.

You might end up in a situation where there isn't a friend in sight.

> 66 I had been really good friends with Megan since second grade. We did everything together. But in fourth grade, Nikki came to school. At first we all three got along, but then Megan and Nikki started getting together and having sleepovers and doing everything without including me. I was really depressed and discouraged. I still tried to be nice to both of them, but it was hard. I got mad one day and asked them why they weren't including me in any of their activities. They didn't really say anything. We didn't talk to each other for a long time. 99

Even if none of that has happened to you, it could, or you'll at least know somebody who has had to go through it. Girl politics are happening all over the tween years (and they always have).

That's why you have this book in your hand right now. I've written it to help you—

- know what REAL friendship looks like (and doesn't look like!).

- fix the "Friendship Flubs" everybody makes because you're, uh, human.

- stay away from the major mistakes like cliques and bullying.

- be a part of making your girl community a place where every girl can be the true self she was made to be.

And just so you know, I've had a lot of help with this book from mini-women who, like you, are making their way through girl politics this very moment. You'll see their totally true stories here, and you'll know you are SO not alone.

Some of my mini-women friends shared their thoughts with me about what makes a true friend. Here's what they said:

- A real friend is a person who sticks with you no matter what, even if another friend comes along.

- A true friend knows you're completely INSANE and loves you anyway.

- A true friend is someone to cry with you when you're hiding out in the bathroom.

- A true BFF loves you more than things.

- A real friend will tell you the truth, even if it hurts.

- A true friend is like family, better than a sister.

- Somebody who is your real friend knows you right down to what you like as pizza toppings.

- For me, a BFF is somebody you don't have to put on an act around.

- A true friend is one who has your back and won't leave you when you're not cool.

66 Why is having friends such a big deal now? When I was little, it didn't matter that much because I was all about my family, but now, like if my BFF is absent from school, I'm totally lost! 99

HERE'S THE DEAL

It's way normal to want close friends and to be completely bummed out if you don't have them or if things don't go that well when you do. Having best buds helps you get some skills you're going to need your whole life:

- Treating people right so they'll love you when they don't **have** to (like your family does).

- Feeling safe with people outside your own family.

- Knowing what kind of people you want to hang out with—and what kind aren't good for you.

- Discovering what you're like when things don't go the way you want.

- Figuring out how to settle arguments or not have them every ten minutes.

That's why it's not only fun, but it's also important to have friends!

66 Your best friend just gets you. 99

66 She loves you when you're hurt emotionally, even if being hurt makes her hurt too. **99**

66 She's somebody who gives you warmth when you're in a bad mood. **99**

Who, ME?

Write YOUR definition of a true friend.

_____

_____

_____

_____

_____

66 A true friend will help you when you're doing the wrong thing and need direction. **99**

66 If my best friend and I have fights and stuff, does that mean we aren't really best friends? **99**

Who, ME?

Check off the things on the below list that have happened to YOU.

No relationship is perfect. (Have you noticed?) Certain things go down in every friendship and girl group:

- ○ A girl is accidentally left out.

- ○ An old friend kind of drifts away to other friends or activities.

- ○ Arguments and splits happen, and then everybody gets back together (sometimes within the same hour!).

- ○ Feelings get hurt without anybody meaning for it to happen, like name-calling for fun.

- ○ People sometimes get jealous.

- ○ Friends get annoyed with each other. (Imagine that!)

- ○ A girl doesn't fit into one group for some reason, so she finds another one.

- ○ You realize a friendship is bad for you, and you have to break it off. (Don't you hate that?)

That's all normal stuff. It's *hard* normal stuff, but it gives you a chance to learn how to work things out with people. We'll talk about those "Friendship Flubs" in chapter 3.

Just So You Know

Girls who surround themselves with good friends are less likely to be bullied.

Sometimes, though, the things that go on between girls aren't "just a normal part of growing up." No matter what some people might tell you, there are things said and done on purpose to make a girl feel really horrible about herself.

- You can't sit here. This seat's taken.

- Didn't you already wear that outfit this week?

- I'm gonna tell her she can't come to my sleepover after all. I just don't like her anymore.

- My mom's making me invite her, but we're all going to ditch her the whole time.

- Haven't you ever heard of deodorant?

- If you keep hanging out with her, none of us will be your friends anymore.

- I heard—from somebody who totally knows—that she's already kissed a guy.

- Hey, girls, look who ate an entire village this summer!

Faithgirlz Journal

My Doodles, Dreams and Devotion

Looking for a place to dream, doodle, and record your innermost questions and secrets? You will find what you seek within the pages of the Faithgirlz Journal, which has plenty of space for you to discover who you are, explore who God is shaping you to be, or write down whatever inspires you. Each journal page has awesome quotes and powerful Bible verses to  encourage you on your walk with God! So grab a pen, colored pencils, or even a handful of markers. Whatever you write is just between you and God.

Available in stores and online!

NIV Faithgirlz! Bible, Revised Edition

Nancy Rue

Every girl wants to know she's totally unique and special. This Bible says that with Faithgirlz! sparkle. Through the many in-text features found only in the Faithgirlz! Bible, girls will grow closer to God as they discover the journey of a lifetime.

Features include:

- Book introductions—Read about the who, when, where, and what of each book.

- Dream Girl—Use your imagination to put yourself in the story.

- Bring It On!—Take quizzes to really get to know yourself.

- Is There a Little (Eve, Ruth, Isaiah) in You?—See for yourself what you have in common.

- Words to Live By—Check out these Bible verses that are great for memorizing.

- What Happens Next?—Create a list of events to tell a Bible story in your own words.

- Oh, I Get It!—Find answers to Bible questions you've wondered about.

- The complete NIV translation

- Features written by bestselling author Nancy Rue

Available in stores and online!

Talk It Up!

Want free books?
First looks at the best new fiction?
Awesome exclusive merchandise?

We want to hear from you!

Give us your opinions on titles, covers, and stories.
Join the Z Street Team.

Email us at zstreetteam@zondervan.com
to sign up today!

Also—Friend us on Facebook!

Find us on
Facebook

www.facebook.com/goodteenreads

• Video Trailers

• Connect with your favorite authors

• Sneak peeks at new releases

• Giveaways

• Fun discussions

• And much more!

ZONDERVAN®
.com